Co-Parenting With a Narcissist

A Life-Changing Guide to Set Boundaries, Protect Your Child From Parental Alienation, and Preserve Your Sanity

Melanie Parker

© Copyright 2023 – Melanie Parker – All rights reserved

The content within this book may not be reproduced, duplicated, or transmitted without direct written permission from the author or the publisher.

Under no circumstances will any blame or legal responsibility be held against the publisher, or author, for any damages, reparation, or monetary loss due to the information contained within this book, either directly or indirectly.

Legal Notice

This book is copyright protected. It is only for personal use. You cannot amend, distribute, sell, use, quote, or paraphrase any part, or the content within this book, without the consent of the author-publisher.

Disclaimer Notice

Please note that the information contained within this document is for educational and entertainment purposes only. All effort has been executed to present accurate, up-to-date, and reliable, complete information. No warranties of any kind are declared or implied. Readers acknowledge that the author is not engaging in rendering legal, financial, medical, or professional advice.

Table of Contents

Introduction 4

Chapter 1: A Closer Look at Narcissism 6

Chapter 2: Is Your Partner a Narcissist? 17

Chapter 3: Narcissistic People - How to Handle Them 25

Chapter 4: How to Deal With Narcissistic Temper Tantrums and Rage 31

Chapter 5: Divorcing a Narcissist 36

Chapter 6: Child Development and Adapting to Parental Separation 43

Chapter 7: Basic Rules for Successful Co-Parenting 53

Chapter 8: Establishing Co-Parenting Goals 62

Chapter 9: Effective Co-Parenting Strategies 66

Chapter 10: How to Co-Parent Without Arguing 72

Chapter 11: Co-Parenting with a Narcissist Parent 75

Chapter 12: Set Boundaries When Co-Parenting With a Narcissist 83

Chapter 13: The Challenges of Co-Parenting With a Narcissist 87

Chapter 14: Parallel Parenting - A Safer Alternative to Co-Parenting? 92

Chapter 15: The Effects of Narcissistic Abuse on Your Kids 97

Chapter 16: Parental Alienation - A Form of Emotional Child Abuse 104

Chapter 17: Protecting and Making it Easier for Your Child 110

Chapter 18: Empathy Parenting - What You Should Know 117

Chapter 19: Strategies for Healthy Emotional Regulation 121

Chapter 20: Mental Health – The Importance of the Expert 126

Chapter 21: What You Should Learn From This Relationship 129

Conclusion 134

Author's Note 138

Introduction

As a parent, you may want to start by reading this book or e-book to determine if your spouse has narcissistic tendencies. Understanding the signs and characteristics of narcissism can be very difficult and requires time and patience. In addition, your desire to explore the possibilities is a positive step if you have a borderline personality disorder and are looking for a treatment plan to help yourself or your child.

The dangers of narcissistic parents may be present in the lack of empathy they express, their lack of ability to understand boundaries, and their ability to manipulate without consideration for their child's emotional well-being. When narcissism is present in a parent, narcissistic personality disorder contributes to these traits. Children whose parents have personality disorders are often subjected to emotional and psychological torment. Emotional abuse and control are common for children who must navigate emotional and social dangers daily.

This book aims to provide a rich, emotional narrative of how to survive the possible damage caused by children whose parent is narcissistic. Narcissists view themselves as being better than everyone else; if you think about it, this makes sense from their point of view. They have constantly been told that they are unique for one reason or another. It is the only way they have ever known, so there is no reason to think anything has changed just because you have come into their lives. They are self-absorbed and often put others down to feel better about themselves.

What are the best options when dealing with someone so focused on themselves that they place no value on your feelings or well-being? What can you do when you feel alone in this battle, and no one understands your daily struggles? How do they become so controlling? It is not all about you. You likely have been dealing with this feeling of isolation for years. You probably made excuses for your spouse, lied to yourself, and denied that anything was wrong. Before you can heal, you must stop lying to yourself and confront the problem. After reading several books on this subject, you must face that your spouse will never love you as much as they love themself, nor will they ever change. They will never be the person you thought you married. Once you acknowledge the problem and accept it, you will feel a sense of relief.

Chapter 1:
A Closer Look at Narcissism

A narcissist is a manipulative, self-centered person with little empathy for others. They constantly compare themselves with others, never take the time to listen to others, and are incredibly demanding. Narcissists are also very bossy and believe they know better than others. They do not value individuality and will often make demands on their partners based on their looks and social standing.

Narcissists need constant affirmation and praise to fuel their egos. Often, they will make situations up to earn recognition from others. They will ask countless questions of others and create unnecessary drama to receive attention and validation.

Grandiose Narcissism

Grandiose narcissism is a type of narcissism. It is characterized by inflated self-esteem and overconfidence. These people are prone to make irrational decisions and are not easily convinced by the opinions of others. They are impulsive and tend to make illogical decisions even when unsure of the consequences.

Grandiose narcissists often find another source of narcissistic supply outside their relationship. They may try to create a perfect family with their new partner. They may also introduce their new partner to their children too soon or bring them to events inappropriately.

The narcissist's victim mentality is rooted in their sense of victimhood; they cannot see themselves as anything but victims. They feel bad only when their decisions backfire or no longer serve their interests.

People who adopt this mindset feel justified in doing terrible things to their targets. This mindset is very harmful to one's health and a relationship. People who are victimized tend to have low self-esteem. Narcissists purposefully play the victim role to gain attention or manipulate other people.

Pathological Narcissism

Pathological narcissism is a serious personality disorder often linked with other mental health problems. Pathological narcissists struggle to control their emotions and behaviors, and they may not be able to adapt to changes in their environment. The condition can lead to depression and other physical problems.

This disorder affects relationships in many ways. It can affect a person's physical well-being and, in extreme cases, even lead to self-harming behaviors, including substance abuse. The narcissist may become violent with their domestic partner. In addition, pathological narcissism can affect relationships and lead to infidelity.

The Characteristics of Narcissists

In recent years, the prevalence of narcissism has significantly increased, with a 30% increase reported in a study of university students between 1979 and 2006. They may experience shame but do not feel guilt and take no responsibility for another person's distress.

- **Lack of Emotional Capacity**

Most narcissists are pretentious; they suffer from an inflated sense of superiority that is unrealistic and often accompanied by overestimation of IQ, performance, leadership, attractiveness, and peer ranking.

While narcissists highly value these traits, they do not have the emotional capacity to play an active role in the communal part of relationships. This lack of emotional capacity was noted by researchers in Poland who surveyed 273 university students in 15 groups. They also gave the participants personality tests and asked them to rate the people in their groups.

The results showed that a lack of emotional capacity among narcissistic people might be related to the frequency of these characteristics. These individuals may be vulnerable to various emotional situations threatening their health. They may also have difficulties controlling their emotions, resulting in emotional dysregulation.

- **Sense of Entitlement**

A sense of entitlement is a personality trait based on the belief that people should be able to get what they want. This entitlement makes people feel the world owes them something, regardless of the circumstances. For example, if a child is given anything they want, they will grow up expecting the same treatment from adults. Certain personality disorders may also cause this trait.

They project their faults and shortcomings onto others and become angry when people do not fulfill their wishes. If you have a narcissist as a partner, you will have to be prepared to endure this type of behavior.

- **Lack of Empathy**

Narcissistic individuals have lower empathy levels than the average person. This association is consistent across the sex spectrum and various demographics. It has also been observed in community and clinical samples of both sexes. However, the exact mechanism by which narcissism impairs empathy is unclear.

While empathy may be hereditary, research suggests that a person's upbringing, parenting, and culture may influence their level of empathy. A lack of empathy is often a tipping point toward toxic narcissism. However, research indicates that empathy in narcissists may reveal other traits, such as emotional intolerance.

A person who lacks empathy can be difficult to recognize because they do not feel compassion for others' feelings. However, it is possible to spot the lack of empathy among narcissists by observing their behavior. While they often behave in ways that are not considerate of others, they seem to know what others like and dislike. They tend to be antisocial, physically abusive, and commit crimes.

- **Lack of Understanding of Feelings**

When dealing with a narcissist, be very cautious about your responses. Typically, a narcissist will avoid emotional interaction and seek to avoid conflict. They may withdraw from others, resent attention, or be insensitive. These symptoms can result in interpersonal conflicts, fluctuating self-esteem, and underlying insecurity.

The lack of understanding among narcissists is one of the most frustrating aspects of their interpersonal relationships. These people often take on a victim role when they feel that someone else is putting their feelings in danger. Alternatively, they may ignore feedback.

- **Need for Admiration**

The narcissist's need for admiration is a key sign of the personality disorder. Narcissists often believe they are better than everyone else and expect praise even when they have not done anything to deserve it.

This lack of self-awareness can lead them to exaggerate their accomplishments and misrepresent their talents. They also talk about their greatness and how lucky people are to have them. However, despite their high self-esteem and need for praise, narcissists often feel empty inside and need admiration to chase away this feeling.

Narcissistic disorders are often hidden and covert. Females display a greater degree of covert narcissism than their male counterparts due to the high importance placed on the physical appearance of females in today's culture.

Narcissists also internalize a profound sense of shame or insecurity and are particularly sensitive to criticism and failure. They may react with contempt or anger. They may also attempt to avoid situations where they can fail, despite the possibility that they may lose their sense of self-importance.

- **Exaggeration**

Exaggeration is one of the common symptoms of narcissism. Narcissists often exaggerate their accomplishments and talents to gain more attention and appreciation. This behavior feeds the narcissist's unrealistic fantasies of power, success, and beauty, leading to excessive arrogance. These behaviors can make it difficult for a narcissist to accept criticism or feedback, often leading to relationships and employment problems.

Narcissists have a low tolerance for criticism and fail to understand how others feel. They cannot identify with their suffering and tend to blame others.

- **Lying**

One of the major symptoms of narcissism is lying. Narcissists use this type of behavior to mask their true feelings. They have a hard time admitting to wrongdoing and lack whole-object relations. While they may apologize for their actions, they rarely mean them.

Narcissists score low on the HEXACO Personality Inventory assessment, which measures six personality traits. Narcissists have low scores on the honesty-humility dimension and demonstrate low scores in sincerity, fairness, and greed avoidance.

Narcissists are good at making promises. They may promise to do things they dislike or do better than they do. They may also promise to do something for others even if they are not happy doing them.

The Origins of Narcissism

The concept of narcissism has been recognized throughout history. However, the word was not coined until the nineteenth century. The term refers to the character Narcissus.

Narcissus is a mythical figure from ancient Greek mythology. The story is about a river god who fathered a beautiful nymph. After receiving a message from a prophet that he would live until old age, Narcissus fell in love with his reflection in a spring stream. As a result, he spent hours gazing at his reflection until he was enamored with it.

Early life is a formative time for a child's self-development. The mother's interactions with the child help shape the child's self-image. Empathetic, nurturing parents encourage this development.

- **Parental Overvaluation**

Parental overvaluation may be a source of narcissistic behavior in children. Overvaluation occurs when a parent has an unrealistic view of the child and focuses too much attention on their qualities. For example, a parent may overclaim their child's knowledge or skills and praise them excessively.

Studies have linked the development of narcissism with parental overvaluation. In one study, parents were asked what topics their children should know. Parents who overvalued their children said their children should know about issues that did not exist. These parents then set their children up to become narcissistic later in life.

- **Early Socialization Experiences**

Early socialization experiences are an important factor in determining narcissism's development. During this period, a child develops an internalized sense of worth and value. This view of self is the foundation of self-esteem. This belief is reinforced by parental overvaluation and overconfidence.

Adolescence is often the first significant socialization experience outside of families. Studies have shown that friendships rank high on adolescents' lists of priorities. However, socialization is also affected by parental influence.

- **Self-Centeredness in Childhood**

Children who are overindulged and are exposed to overly indulgent environments are at a greater risk of developing narcissism later in life.

These inflated perceptions of their worth are often defense mechanisms against an underlying fear of being unlovable.

- **Relationships With Others**

Narcissism is a personality disorder that has its roots in relationships with others. It is considered a developmental disorder and does not become apparent to outsiders until a person is well into their 20s. During this time, a person's relationship with others ruptures and becomes tumultuous.

Narcissists have a hard time understanding the feelings of others. As a result, they view others as objects and do not place the needs of others above their own. Because of this, they can take advantage of people without thinking twice about it. Their lack of empathy also means they do not realize that their behavior negatively affects others.

Narcissism treatment begins with an understanding of the underlying causes. Patients with narcissism have fragile self-esteem and need constant affirmation and validation from others. In addition, insults to their "grandiose self" can cause feelings of rejection and shame.

Narcissistic clients often seek treatment after their idealized image is dashed when something unexpected happens, resulting in depression or a midlife crisis for the narcissist. Narcissistic personality disorder often co-occurs with co-morbid mood disorders, including major depression and dysthymia.

The Effects of Narcissism

Narcissism can have a range of negative effects on relationships. In addition to interpersonal relationships, it can affect a person's confidence and decision-making.

- **Relationships**

Narcissists can have a profound effect on the lives of those around them. They can make even the simplest decisions that seem complicated, leaving their victims feeling worthless. A narcissist is generally uncooperative, cold, and abusive to others. They can be cruel and unreliable, and their partners often find themselves torn between love and pain. Their partners often ignore their feelings and do not give them any credit.

- **Decision Making**

Recent research has found that people with grandiose narcissism have poor decision-making. In one study, 252 Americans with an average age of 36 completed a narcissistic personality assessment and a hypothetical decision-making scenario. The subjects were shown expert estimates and allowed to alter their answers.

CEO narcissism is positively related to decision speed but negatively associated with decision comprehensiveness. Narcissists seek competitive situations that will prove their superiority and elevate their status.

- **Confidence**

Narcissistic behavior is often accompanied by overconfidence, and narcissists may even radiate a sense of superiority or entitlement and make risky decisions. As a result, higher narcissism correlates with higher levels of overconfidence.

Overconfidence and narcissism have gained considerable attention in organizational and economic research. Many studies have shown that overconfidence and narcissism may negatively affect sales variance, corporate fraud, and capital structure. While these studies have mostly focused on the negative aspects of CEO over-confidence, some have also found that overconfidence can be beneficial.

- **Impulsivity**

A recent study analyzed the relationship between narcissism and impulsivity. It found that impulsivity does not affect decision accuracy but does increase participants' likelihood of externalizing blame. The study also analyzed the role of narcissism in influencing confidence and using experts.

In addition, narcissists tend to form shallow interpersonal relationships with other people. They use these relationships primarily as ways to promote their image. They do not place much value on others, and they may violently react when relationships fail.

- **Addiction to Self-Improvement**

Although narcissism is associated with adolescent substance use disorders, it is unclear if this phenomenon also occurs in adults. Moreover, studies that recruit normative adolescents dominate the literature on narcissism. Therefore, further research is needed to explore the effects of narcissistic behaviors on substance use among adolescents.

Narcissism symptoms include a desire for attention and a need to improve one's life. To achieve their goals, narcissists spend a great deal of time enhancing their appearances and gaining admiration from others. As a result, their need for attention grows, similar to an addict's addiction to a new high. Furthermore, they suffer deep depression and great anxiety if they fail to receive the attention they crave.

Narcissistic individuals are often vulnerable, which increases their risk of depression. This vulnerability amplifies unpleasant mental states, diverting resources from adaptive responses. Pathological grandiosity is also linked to depression as it leads to feelings of failure, loneliness, lack of accomplishment, and isolation and can trigger depression.

- **Anxiety**

The fear of criticism and humiliation is a recurring theme in the lives of narcissists. These people often cannot function normally in social settings because they fear rejection. These fears are common to those suffering from anxiety disorders.

Chapter 2:
Is Your Partner a Narcissist?

If you are living with someone who has a narcissistic personality disorder, it is important to understand that you are not alone and that there are several ways to deal with this personality disorder. Getting help can be difficult; you may not be willing to seek assistance because you feel it is a personal attack. However, it is important to remember that narcissists do not mean to hurt you personally, and their actions and mistakes are never your fault.

How to Tell a Narcissist From a Normal Person

If you are curious to know how to tell a narcissist from a normal person, there are several signs of which to be aware. Narcissists feel threatened when they are not the focus of attention. They also lack empathy and rarely acknowledge the suffering of others.

- **Narcissists Expect Praise**

Narcissists are self-absorbed and selfish, expecting praise and recognition from others to feel appreciated. They do not give much thought to other people's feelings and will pout when they are told "no." Narcissists are rarely compassionate and have a limited understanding of other people's feelings. In addition, they often think their feelings result from other people's behavior, so they are unlikely to offer apologies or comfort.

Narcissists also tend to be deceptive and will do anything to get praise. They often manipulate love relationships to achieve their own goals and objectives. They will make others feel bad about themselves when they do not deserve it and disparage others to keep them in the relationship.

Narcissists will not listen to what you have to say and are not likely to care about your opinions. While they will not show empathy, narcissists often feel threatened and act as if they have been attacked. As a result, a narcissist's reaction to a negative situation may be a rage-inducing response.

- **Narcissists Feel Threatened by People Who Do Not Kowtow to Them**

A narcissist feels threatened when people do not kowtow to them and do not follow their every whim. As a result, they often act aggressively when people ask for help or do not kowtow to them. Because of their lack of empathy, a narcissist is unable to understand the feelings of others truly and views people as objects rather than people. When narcissists feel threatened, they often lash out in anger and contempt, further boosting their ego.

Narcissists interpret everything as a personal attack. They feel threatened by anything and everything that might make them look bad. They do not realize they are not the only ones harmed by narcissism.

- **Narcissists Have a Fantasy World Mentality**

The narcissist has a worldview completely devoid of empathy or concern for others. They make up stories, embellish their appearances, and associate with high-profile people to maintain this fantasy. They may even claim to be movie stars or millionaires and may have adoring fans. Whenever someone challenges their inflated sense of superiority, they will launch a tirade.

Narcissists use their fantasy world to justify their antisocial behavior. They create unrealistic expectations and punish failures. It is hard to tell whether the narcissist has any true values. Narcissists also have no memory of past events.

A narcissist's fantasy world is based on the idea that they deserve everything and should be treated like a celebrity. As a result, they expect others to comply with their every whim automatically. They also tend to lie about their talents and exaggerate their achievements to ensure they will be seen as the "one" who deserves it all. This way of thinking can make the narcissist feel important and valuable. It also reinforces that they are the center of attention and that other people merely bit players.

- **Narcissists Have Low Self-Esteem**

Narcissists are not only self-centered but also very fragile and can use their low self-esteem to cause great harm to others. While they will change behavior if necessary to achieve their goal, these efforts are temporary. Narcissists will often try to make others feel bad about themselves through their actions and are quick to blame others for their mistakes. They may also brag about their successes yet fail to acknowledge others' achievements.

Although narcissists may show external signs of low self-esteem, they do not necessarily have it. They do not want to show their insecurities to others. They simply use other people to validate their fragile egos and keep them happy.

When narcissists' fragile self-esteem crumbles, they experience extreme defensiveness and aggressive, hostile reactions. They are notorious liars and abuse others' belief in them. They use their false sense of importance to gain self-esteem and adoration. They often deny they have self-esteem issues and are the best at believing their own lies.

How to Recognize the Narcissist's Manipulation

Recognizing the strategies a narcissist will use is crucial for surviving their manipulation. Although they may look like givers, narcissists are incredibly manipulative and take advantage of those they manipulate. They often devalue their victims to the point of degrading them.

- **Narcissists Are Not Givers**

Narcissists manipulate their victims in many ways, some more obvious than others. Overt narcissists brag about themselves and drag you down. They are not the kind to show their emotions when they do something nice. They take over your conversations and make you feel bad.

If you suspect a person of being a narcissist, there are a few signs to keep in mind. The first sign is gaslighting, which makes the other person feel stupid and worthless. They use this technique to make the victim doubt their thoughts, memories, past actions, and sanity.

- **Narcissists Take Advantage of Others**

In many ways, the behavior of a narcissist resembles a sadist. Narcissists often use dangerous and degrading language to lure victims into a trap. They may even try to persuade their victims that they were the victims of the situation.

The narcissist deliberately targets vulnerable people. They will often appear charming, friendly, or quirky—all of which is a cover for their deceit. However, when challenged, they quickly become dangerous. They will take their selfishness to new heights, causing damage.

- **Narcissists Manipulate**

One of the biggest signs of narcissism is constant manipulation. For example, narcissists may send text messages or create distressing online posts designed to make their victims question their thoughts or sanity. They may even make the victim feel guilty or sorry for the narcissist's problems.

- **Narcissists Devalue Victims**

A narcissist is a dangerous person who manipulates his or her victims. These people want to make the victims feel worthless, which can have devastating psychological effects. In some cases, victims may suffer from traumatic experiences and mental disorders.

Symptoms of narcissistic behavior can range from repeated accusations to blaming others when things go wrong. The narcissist may also say, "Thanks for taking out the trash," even though he or she did it. These repeated behaviors can be disorienting to the victim. Narcissists may also say that they never have problems outside of the relationship.

- **Narcissists Employ Triangulation**

Narcissists use subtle language and changes in tone to gain control over their victims. They will use words to create a false sense of intimacy, then use these words later to reopen old wounds.

In addition, a narcissist will use a third party to control the situation. This tactic is called triangulation, and it involves involving a third party in communication channels. This tactic is often used to make the victim feel jealous or guilty.

- **Narcissists Make Their Victims Dependent on Them**

The narcissist will create an illusion of dependency in their victims, often using lies and fear. Eventually, this dependency will turn into a nightmare scenario, and the victim will be vulnerable to the narcissist's manipulation and agenda.

A typical narcissist will use their body to dominate and invade their victim's personal space. They will also use subtle language to intimidate their victims. Moreover, they will sabotage their relationships, often under the guise of humor, revenge, or personal advantage. Narcissists enjoy putting the victim on the defensive and making them feel guilty about problems. They may even threaten their victims with harm, particularly to children.

Long-Term Damages Incurred From Being in a Narcissistic Relationship

There are some long-term damages resulting from being in a narcissistic relationship. These include PTSD, a lack of spontaneity, and the loss of your divine self. In addition, being in a narcissistic relationship can lead to an increased risk of depression and an overall sense of negativity and anxiety.

- **Post-Traumatic Stress Disorder (PTSD)**

Being in a narcissistic relationship can be very damaging. The abuse may be ongoing rather than a one-time event. For this reason, healing from narcissistic abuse may take time.

Narcissists are extremely manipulative, and they can manipulate your sense of reality. Narcissistic relationships are emotionally draining, and you may need to learn healthy ways to deal with your emotions. Narcissists tend to avoid trying new things because they worry they will fail. They also worry about their status and power. They feel powerless when they are not in control.

A narcissist will rarely, if ever, express his or her genuine feelings. They feel superior to their partners and view emotional attachments as a sign of weakness. They may even fake their feelings to gain attention. They do not like crying because it means nurturing the other person, which they do not want you to do.

- **Loss of Divine Self**

The first step in healing from a narcissistic relationship is recognizing the parts of yourself that the abuser has distorted. Narcissists often mirror the personas of their victims, reflecting their projections of fulfillment, beauty, divinity, and ecstasy. Once you notice this pattern, you will be ready to leave the relationship.

A narcissist experiences the world around them as a film they watch from the sidelines, with little or no control over the outcome. The narcissist does not remember how he or she felt at any given moment and often is only dimly aware of the battle raging within because they have severed the connection between their emotions and cognition. This disconnect results in a person feeling sad, depressed, and suicidal, with no outside reason for the feelings.

- **Psychological Cage**

When you are in a relationship with a narcissist, you must be aware of the psychological cage they are creating for you. Narcissists do not respond well to typical boundaries. Rather, they have a life-long quest for security and validation.

Dealing with a narcissist is not easy. Their constant need for adoration and validation leaves their victims tired and insecure. As a result, they engage in various attention-seeking behaviors to gain your attention. The more attention they get, the more you will become dependent on them.

Chapter 3:
Narcissistic People - How to Handle Them

The best way to handle a narcissist is to analyze the situation objectively and retain your emotional balance. Avoid engaging in the blame game. Narcissists use illogical arguments to convince you that you are at fault. Their arguments change frequently and can be tricky to decipher.

- **Dispassionately Analyzing a Narcissist Restores Emotional Balance**

Analyzing a narcissist requires a collaborative approach to determine the goals of treatment. This process must start with validating the patient's experience to disarm their defensiveness, then balance the validation with clarification and confrontation.

First, it is essential to recognize that narcissists are merely people with a disorder that causes them to perceive reality differently. Often, simple positive statements can counteract their frustration. Alternatively, you can seek an outside perspective to analyze a narcissist's behavior.

Recognizing the narcissist's motives for behavior is imperative, especially when it involves a work setting. They may seek to impress superiors or other people through their work or use other people to get their way in the workplace.

Understanding the motivational processes involved in empathy can be difficult for individuals close to a narcissist. However, a proactive approach to understanding these feelings will replace the stigma associated with these individuals.

- **Avoiding the Blame Game**

When dealing with a narcissistic person, avoid playing the blame game. The narcissist will try to play the victim card to win your pity. They will often emphasize their victimization so that their faults will seem smaller. The narcissist's primary tool is manipulation. They are good at knowing their victims' emotional states and can manipulate them with their words and actions.

It is crucial to remember that narcissists often turn to other people to manipulate you. Avoiding the blame game will allow you to keep the conversation on track and avoid making yourself look bad.

Avoid the blame game by not taking responsibility for the narcissist's behavior. Narcissists cannot take responsibility for their actions and will instead attempt to shift the blame onto others. Another name for this behavior is blame shifting, a common tactic used by narcissists to maintain control over their victims.

Avoid the blame game by not blaming the narcissist for the actions of others. If you are constantly blaming the narcissist for a mishap, the narcissist is not making any sense, and your efforts are not helping the situation. Instead, try to understand how they got into this state and how you can help them change their behavior.

- **Avoiding Gossip**

Narcissists enjoy starting gossip, so it is crucial to avoid gossip when dealing with them. They may try to wreak havoc in the workplace by spreading rumors and inciting workplace gossip. If you are one of the people who work with a narcissist, it is best to avoid gossiping about them and avoid personal conversations with them. Office gossip can be harmful to the morale of your entire workplace.

Narcissists also use gossip to gain sympathy and create a falsely intimate environment. They may tell ridiculous stories, even if they are not true. They might even pretend to have a mental health condition or a substance abuse problem to manipulate you into believing them. Narcissists are highly sophisticated and are constantly learning new tricks to manipulate others.

- **Avoiding Venting**

One way to avoid venting when dealing with narcissism is to avoid raising your voice. Doing so only escalates the narcissist's rage. To prevent this behavior, keep your voice low and avoid making threats.

Remaining calm will help disarm the narcissist and stop the escalation of the situation. Narcissists often take credit for things that are done by others. They usually try to manipulate the situation by making up stories to gain sympathy and intimacy.

- **Avoiding Codependency**

Codependency is a common problem when dealing with narcissists. Because they fear disappointing others, codependents tend to gravitate toward controlling partners. They also have trouble imagining a life without a partner.

On the other hand, narcissists thrive on attention and need others' approval to maintain their inflated egos. When partners do not put up with their excessive pride and insecurity, they become very offended and feel the other person does not appreciate their importance.

- **Performing Acts of Kindness**

One way to recover from narcissistic abuse is to perform daily acts of kindness, which can significantly alter how you think about the world. Narcissists are incapable of understanding and connecting with other people's feelings. They often instruct their victims to hide their feelings and avoid expressing them. These behaviors can also lead to depression, anxiety, and PTSD.

Avoid engaging in narcissistic behaviors while you are in a relationship. Narcissists tend to have very high standards of themselves and expect complete compliance from their partners. They will often pressure you into giving up your interests and friendships to keep up with their demands. If this happens, you should step away from the relationship.

- **Getting Help to Recover From a Narcissist**

Dealing with a narcissist is an emotionally draining experience. Narcissists can be physically and verbally abusive, so seeking help from a mental health professional is essential for your health and well-being. You should seek help and support, whether it is from a therapist, a primary care physician, or an organization specializing in mental health.

Getting help to recover from a narcissistic relationship requires learning how to identify with the feelings of others. Since narcissists are used to caring only about their feelings and opinions, it is important to understand theirs. You need to understand what their pain feels like. Try to imagine what you would feel like in the same situation and how you would react.

The Important Rule When to Cut All Contact

Sometimes, it is difficult to do so after a breakup, but by staying away from your ex for a while, you will gain mental clarity that will allow you to make a rational decision. You will also have a chance to figure out whether you are better off without your ex.

- **Breaking No-Contact Means Breaking Up**

You must first realize that breaking no-contact does not mean you have to forget your ex. It means you need time away from them to process your feelings and heal. The breakup is a natural and necessary process, and you should remember that it is important to remain friendly with your ex even if you do not see or talk to them. You must also keep your mind busy by engaging in other activities and avoiding the things that might bring you back to your ex.

Also, no-contact is a great time to reflect on the relationship and learn from your mistakes. It will serve to help you make fewer mistakes the next time around. You may want to hire a relationship coach or learn to meditate to focus on yourself instead of trying to win your ex back.

- **Signs That No-Contact Is Working**

If you have separated and have not spoken to your ex in months, they are signs that your no-contact rule is working. You may feel tempted to contact your ex, but it is not healthy. It will only add to the stress, frustration, and fear and can lead to neediness and self-sabotage. Instead, stay focused on other aspects of your life and distract yourself from your ex. Just remember to maintain your no-contact rule.

Another sign that your no-contact rule is working is newfound self-love. After all, a breakup should have left you feeling depressed and lonely, and it is healthy to focus on improving yourself. Practicing self-love will help you become more aware of your self-worth and help you improve your physical and emotional health.

- **Timeline**

When it comes to ending a relationship, it can be difficult to know exactly when to cut off all contact. The key to making the right decision is setting boundaries and communicating them to the other person. If you are in a relationship with someone toxic, it may be beneficial to send them a message through another medium.

- **Signs That It Will Not Work**

If you have cut all contact with your ex, you may wonder whether they are still thinking of you. Maybe you have started talking to people online or going on dates with new people. The first sign that your no-contact rule is not working is when you begin to feel like your ex is confused, acting hot and cold, or wallowing regretfully. They may start to reach out more often or stop ignoring you altogether.

If you have been with your ex for a while and recently started flirting with other people, they might be jealous of you. You might see pictures of them with someone of the opposite sex on social media, and they might start chatting about dating.

Your ex may even be tracking your movements online. Even mundane updates you make on social media are being read by your ex. If you are not sure whether your ex is stalking you, try changing your social media settings so they cannot see your updates.

Chapter 4:
How to Deal With Narcissistic Temper Tantrums and Rage

When an individual in your life exhibits behavior akin to that of a two-year-old, a therapist might refer to it as narcissistic rage, but you might refer to it as a narcissistic tantrum. Whatever you want to name them, narcissists have these tantrums when they feel challenged, humiliated, or weak. There is no quick fix in this situation, but below is a comprehensive list of tactics you can employ to deal with a narcissistic rage incident as skillfully as possible.

- **Keep Your Distance and Decline to Offer Them the Attention They Demand**

    If you give in to a narcissist's tantrum, they will likely have more frequent or severe rage attacks because they thrive on attention. Leave them alone so they can experience their fit of anger unattended. Even if they do not decide to end their temper tantrum, you will not have to endure the entire affair.

- **Act Distracted and as Though They Are not Even Having a Temper Outburst**

    This is similar to walking away, but it denies the narcissist even a tiny bit of pleasure in knowing they made you leave. Instead, try ignoring them while still in their presence to make it obvious that you will not follow their lead and will not give in to their temper tantrum.

- **Accept Their Feelings While Criticizing Their Reaction as Inappropriate**

    It is a good idea to acknowledge that a narcissist does truly feel challenged, embarrassed, or powerless during a rage episode. However, it is equally crucial to avoid endorsing or justifying their inappropriate response to these emotions. Be straightforward with them regarding both points.

- **Do Not Be Afraid to Stand Up and Be Heard**

    During their fit of rage, the narcissist may act as if they are trying to suffocate you and will not allow you any room to express your point of view. Without yelling or directly confronting them, state calmly and emphatically that you have the same right to express your point of view as they do.

- **Warn Them of the Consequences of Their Anger Outbursts**

    Narcissists find it extremely difficult to link their behavior to any kind of adverse effect. If you can make them feel this connection, you might be able to manage their tantrum. Be as concise and straightforward as possible while avoiding personal attacks.

- **Solicit Them to See the Circumstance From Your Point of View**

    They may reconsider their behaviors if they try to imagine themselves in your situation. Due to their propensity to only see things from their own point of view, this is a challenging job for narcissists and may not be successful. However, if you can get them to pause and genuinely picture the roles being switched, they might realize that their temper tantrum is inappropriate and unacceptable.

- **Set Limits for the Phrases and Behaviors You Will Not Stand For**

Narcissists frequently believe that everything they do, including yelling at people, is totally acceptable. Setting up clear guidelines for what is and is not acceptable might help them realize that their response to the circumstance is excessive. Even if it does not work this time, you have proven that you are capable of advocating for yourself and are ready to do so.

- **Establish Repercussions for the Future and Maintain Them**

There needs to be no doubt about the relationship: their actions will have the precise effects you mention. Additionally, it is crucial that you genuinely mean what you state. The narcissist will repeatedly call your bluff and feel free to have tantrums if you set up repercussions but do not carry them out.

- **Refuse to Lower Yourself to Their Level and Justify Their Actions**

When someone is narcissistically angry at you, it can be very tempting to react to them with some anger of your own. However, you will discover that trying to "out-tantrum" a narcissist will only lead to further escalation of the situation. Instead, make every effort to maintain your composure.

- **Do Not Accept Responsibility Just to Placate Them**

    By falling for the narcissist's trap, you are teaching them that temper outbursts are effective and should be used frequently to get their way. Even though it might seem like a simple solution, by choosing another course of action, you might persuade them that their temper outbursts are ineffective against you.

- **If You Believe Your Safety Is in Danger, Take Precautions**

    Although narcissistic anger episodes are frequently more self-focused, they can occasionally escalate into instances of verbal or physical abuse of others. If you experience verbal or physical abuse, or you believe it is about to happen, get out of there as soon as you can and seek assistance.

- **After Having Their Fit of Anger, Calm Down**

    The emotional toll of narcissistic rage is great. You might feel irate, upset, perplexed, or some mixture of these emotions. Take care of yourself by engaging in self-care practices that are effective for you.

    - Consult a buddy; a trustworthy and attentive person in whom you can place your confidence. Feel free to rant and express yourself. Allow their compassion and encouragement to heal you.

- Be grateful. It can be difficult to keep in mind your blessings when dealing with a narcissist. Make a list of five or ten things for which you are grateful, then take some time to think about it. Make this a daily ritual for continuing advantages.

- Attend counseling sessions. Even though narcissists are rarely willing to attend therapy, it can be very beneficial for individuals like you who work with narcissists. The counselor can assist you in identifying and creating unique coping mechanisms.

Chapter 5:
Divorcing a Narcissist

Divorcing a narcissist can be difficult as they are prone to extreme behavior. Some of the most common involve dragging out the process, demanding a "perfect" image, or avoiding divorce altogether.

- **Narcissists Are Prone to Extreme Behavior**

Divorcing a narcissist prone to extreme behavior may seem daunting, but there are ways to make the process easier. Narcissists are often cunning and exploit their spouse's weaknesses to gain control. They may attempt to take the children from their partners during a divorce and will lie to get what they want. They will try to win every argument.

While divorce can be a very stressful time for anyone, the process can be made easier by preparing yourself for the extreme behavior a narcissist is prone to display.

Learn to identify the signs and symptoms of gaslighting. If you find yourself dealing with this behavior repeatedly, seek therapy to help you handle the situation better.

Narcissists are often not emotionally intelligent and cannot relate to other people. They will try to manipulate you by claiming to understand your feelings and twisting the truth to make you feel guilty. If your spouse is narcissistic, you may have trouble convincing them that divorce is best for the children.

- **Narcissists Drag Out the Process**

Divorcing a narcissist can be complicated, and a good divorce attorney is essential. While you may feel you can negotiate a divorce, you must be prepared for a lengthy and drawn-out process.

A narcissist is unwilling to compromise and empathize with others. They likely will not consider your best interests or the best interests of your children, making the divorce process very difficult, especially if you have children.

Narcissists drag out the process by filing motions and requesting more time. They also tend to retell stories about their marriage to stall the process. If the divorce proceedings draw out unnecessarily, you may feel vulnerable and confused.

- **Narcissists Demand a Perfect Image**

For divorce from a narcissist to proceed smoothly, you will need some information to use against them.

These individuals are highly controlling and require constant validation. They have no regard for their partners and are more interested in themselves than others. As a result, they do everything they can to make themselves look perfect, even going so far as to slander their former spouse.

Narcissists must project an ideal image, and divorce will likely shatter this. They cannot cope with the loss of control and will often attempt to create as much chaos as possible.

- **Narcissists Are Prone to Drama**

If you are contemplating divorce, it is crucial to realize that it will be a stressful time for you and your spouse. Narcissists are notorious for their drama-filled behaviors and are likely to try to make the process as difficult as possible. They may even create problems to distract you from the real issues.

One of the most important things to do to ensure that your divorce is as simple as possible is to keep detailed records of all your dealings. This way, you can quickly end any drama with indisputable facts about what transpired. It is also a good idea to keep your communication with your narcissist to a minimum, so they will not be able to use your words against you.

The Emotional Stages of Separation

Denial and anger are normal emotions that you may experience after separation. They are a protective mechanism to keep you from hurting yourself too much. But when you have just broken up with a narcissistic partner, these feelings can become destructive. To compensate, think about the good things you shared with your partner and how you can carry on with your life.

- **Denial**

The first stage in the grieving process after a relationship breakup is denial. Putting these things off can only prolong your pain.

Despite this, it is important to acknowledge and accept your feelings. You may miss your partner or realize that you want to pursue other goals. Your anger may be a result of the situation or because your partner has left you.

- **Anger**

The emotional stages of separation are often accompanied by anger. Whether directed at yourself or the other party, anger can make it difficult to make rational decisions and come to an amicable agreement. Anger is a powerful emotion that should be dealt with healthily. Try journaling, working out, or talking to a therapist.

You should avoid expressing your anger in front of your children or online. If you find yourself angry, try talking about it with a therapist or divorce coach. In addition, you should give yourself time to express your feelings without being consumed by them. It is important to remember that your emotions will not last for very long.

- **Depression**

People experiencing depression or separation shock can experience a variety of emotions. One minute they may feel comfortable in their new lifestyle, but the next, they may begin crying over memories of their former partner. At other times, they can become enraged when a bad memory surfaces, such as an argument. In such situations, it is crucial to seek help.

Depression after separation is a natural reaction to the end of a close relationship. Often, this process takes time to complete. People may experience significant changes in their sleep patterns, and they may also experience anxiety or low self-esteem. Some may even develop cognitive disorders, which block them from thinking rationally. The first step toward overcoming depression after separation is acceptance.

- **Acceptance**

Regardless of whether the separation has been sudden or gradual, it is possible to reach acceptance through various emotional stages. You may feel overwhelmed and sad during these stages, but they will pass, and you will reach happier days.

Acceptance helps you see the relationship with new eyes. Although you have been trying to make it work, you cannot make it work anymore. When you have reached acceptance, you can arrange your priorities, and the world will feel fresh again.

Breakups are never easy, especially when children are involved. The emotional response will vary from person to person, and it is best to acknowledge that emotions are natural and normal and work through them. For example, if you have recently broken up with your significant other, you may be experiencing anger. In this case, it is important to acknowledge that your feelings are natural and that you are working through them to move on.

- **Spiritual Un-Bonding**

In a divorce, spiritual un-bonding is an emotional stage of the separation process. This stage of separation begins before the decision to divorce is made and is characterized by new behaviors, such as anger and resistance. For example, an emotionally un-bonding spouse might become angry with her husband and walk out of an argument. Another example is a couple who decides to take a solo vacation. The couple also may avoid doing things they feel they have to do for their spouse.

- **Exiting an Abusive Relationship**

It can be scary to leave an abusive relationship, but it is often the healthiest choice. Start by building a support system. Engage in activities outside the home. Use affirmations to help yourself stay positive. Abusers are often very careful to keep a close eye on their partner's activities, and it can be difficult to leave without your partner's knowledge.

How to Get Past Emotional Abuse

If you have experienced emotional abuse by a narcissist, you may wonder how to get past the painful feelings. First, you should seek support from friends and family. You should also consider seeking counseling. Psychotherapy can help you put the abusive relationship in perspective and give you the tools you need to heal. In addition, talking with other victims of emotional abuse can help you realize you are not alone and access healing strategies.

- **Neglect**

When a relationship fails, it can be hard to discern if your partner is neglecting your needs. There may be no tangible or written evidence, but if your partner does not understand your needs, you have to confront them and talk about them. Do not wait until you are desperate to talk about your problems.

Neglect and emotional abuse can be very harmful to the physical and emotional well-being of young people. In both cases, basic needs are unmet, and parents fail to ensure the safety of their children. They also often do not provide an adequate education for their children.

- **Humiliation**

Humiliation can be an extremely destructive and painful form of emotional abuse. It involves a situation where someone shows the victim that they are not worthy of their position and that they are weak, ineffective, or insignificant. Moreover, this type of abuse can provoke feelings of vindictiveness and even anger. In addition, humiliation may result in a sense of extreme anxiety and fear.

- **Undermining**

An emotionally abusive person will make you feel worthless to them. They will often criticize you for your accomplishments and attempt to discredit you. They may also try to put you down by making you feel inferior, claiming to be only joking.

Verbal abuse is one form of emotional abuse that challenges the victim's perceptions and ideas. It also undermines the victim's confidence and self-esteem.

- **Blaming**

Some abusers blame the victim for the abuse and trivialize the victim's feelings and emotions. They will tell the victim they were overreacting or that they have a bad memory. Blaming is a common coping mechanism for abuse victims.

- **Stonewalling**

When a partner refuses to talk about specific issues, they stonewall. This behavior is not productive in a relationship and should be discouraged. If you notice stonewalling in your relationship, you should gently remind your partner that you do not accept it. You can also consider ending the connection if the abuse continues.

Chapter 6:
Child Development and Adapting to Parental Separation

Child development is a complex area. Adversity during a child's developmental years can significantly affect their cognitive abilities. Piaget's theory of child development and Lev Vygotsky's theory of intrinsic development can provide insight into how early adversity may affect children's development.

Children's Cognitive Development

Children's cognitive development is affected by the stressors and adversity they experience. Poor families, for example, may not have the resources to provide stimulating home environments for children. In addition, they may be under a great deal of family stress, which can interfere with the ability of parents to relate positively to their children.

Parents must understand that children need cooperation within their family and environment to continue positive cognitive development. When parents engage in conflict, violence, and blame, their children are more likely to feel guilt, resulting in lower self-esteem and difficulty learning. These problems may require interventions to help children adapt and move on.

- **Piaget's Theory of Cognitive Development**

According to Piaget's theory of cognitive development, children develop in four distinct stages of intelligence: the sensorimotor stage, pre-operation stage, concrete-operational stage, and formal-operational stage.

Development begins at birth, with children interpreting the world around them, to the final stage, beginning at age twelve, where children learn more about how logic impacts their thinking and the world around them.

According to Piaget, knowledge comprises cognitive structures, called schemas, that describe the world. Children construct these schemas through experience, and they modify them through a process known as adaptation. This process is divided into two parts: assimilation, the process by which existing cognitive schemas are modified to suit new experiences, and accommodation.

- **Lev Vygotsky's Theory of Cognitive Development**

Vygotsky's theory of cognitive developmental processes is an important part of the study of child development. His work influenced many contemporary researchers in the Soviet Union. His insights were expanded, empirically tested, and applied in practical applications. They paved the way for many other theories of human development. These theories included cultural-historical activity theory, which drew from Vygotsky's work.

Vygotsky's theory of cognitive developmental processes also includes sociocultural development, focusing on the child's immediate social environment and adult interactions. This theory suggests that children develop first by learning from their immediate environment. It is the foundation of 'scaffolding,' an approach that aims to help children learn how to socialize with others.

Benefits of Having Two Parents at Home

Having two parents at home is good for children, and research shows it boosts self-esteem and overall well-being. It has been shown to have more benefits than having a single parent. Kids from two-parent families are more likely to have a more stable environment, and the two parents will be more involved in their education. These factors are believed to provide overall well-being for a child.

Children raised with two parents are healthier than their counterparts raised by single parents, step-parents, or grandparents. Their physical and dental health is better, and their risk of developing asthma and other conditions is lower. They also miss fewer school days and experience fewer injuries.

Two-parent households are more stable and financially secure and less likely to experience financial stress. The family is less likely to worry about how much money they have, which means better daycare, early education, and college savings. Two parents also have more time for themselves and their children and can go on more dates and vacations as a family.

Importance of a Stable Relationship

Children who are raised in healthy, stable relationships develop resilience, which is a key component of healthy adulthood. They feel safe, supported, and encouraged to take risks. In addition, they are more likely to be responsible, competent, and educated as adults. Parents, teachers, coaches, grandparents, and friends are all wonderful examples of dependable adults who provide a positive environment for children.

Relationships with adults allow children to express themselves and learn how to respond to others. They learn to trust themselves and can work through hard feelings when they arise. Children also learn how to develop empathy and learn to respect others. It is, therefore, crucial to maintaining a stable relationship with your child.

Children can learn a great deal from their parents. A stable relationship helps children lead longer, happier lives and generally improves their overall health. Parents should model healthy relationships for their children and take care of themselves. Children can see that adults can have healthy relationships by modeling this behavior.

Children can sense instability in their parents, which can affect their self-worth and ability to reach their potential. These instability symptoms may manifest themselves in a variety of ways. Children may feel insecure about their caregivers or unsure of their physical safety. As a result, their eating habits, school performance, and relationships may become altered. Ultimately, children should live with both parents if possible.

Effects of Early Adversity on Children's Development

Adverse events like parental separation and divorce affect children differently and can affect their development and health trajectory. The impact of adversity often depends on the frequency, timing, and duration of exposure.

Adversity can cause traumatic effects on children. When a child experiences a stressful event, that will cause the body's immune system to respond with high-stress hormones. Over time, this excessive activity will wear down the child's body and brain. As a result, adversity can cause a child to experience more difficulties than they would have otherwise.

Attachment Styles

Understanding the different attachment styles is an important first step in addressing the effects of parental separation on children. The separation and divorce process involving a narcissist often results in an acrimonious custody battle, which can negatively affect a child's attachment style.

Children form strong bonds with their primary caregivers and seek physical intimacy with these key attachment figures. When separated from these attachment figures, they experience anxiety. Attachment forms the basis of future interpersonal relationships and gives children the security to explore the world around them. Over time, children develop their sense of self and learn to distinguish signals from their primary caregivers.

Parents can minimize psychological distress for their children by adopting intentional parenting strategies. These strategies aim to alleviate the pressure parents unknowingly place on their children.

Effects of Divorce on Child's Mood and Psyche

Children affected by a divorce experience deep sadness and often lose interest in life. This sadness can be uncontrollable and lead to depression. Older children may even blame themselves for the divorce. Children also suffer from increased stress because of a lack of communication between parents.

While divorce can affect children of any age, young children are most vulnerable to the effects of separation. They may become addicted to substances or engage in destructive behavior. They may also develop physical issues like smoking or prescription drug use. In addition, children may become more prone to illness and show signs of depression.

Although divorce may be upsetting, children do adjust. They can learn how to handle conflicts and will work to avoid them in the future. They may even improve their grades. However, they should not be exposed to the conflict between their parents.

Teenagers, in particular, need parental guidance. If they feel that their parents are paying attention to them, they are less likely to act out or engage in substance use, and they will do better in school. Encouragement from parents will also help children feel better about themselves. They may develop a criminal mindset if their parents do not encourage them.

Skill Training for Children

Skill training for children can begin at an early age. Taking part in physical activities, such as sports, helps children develop social skills that will be useful throughout their lives. In addition, participating in music lessons helps children develop their musical skills while creating a passion for an activity. Parents can help their children develop these skills through many different activities.

It seems that shy children can become more outgoing, aggressive children can learn self-control, and more socially withdrawn children can learn to make friends. Children with better social skills benefit from the rewards of positive relationships and are better able to deal with life's challenges.

Besides improving their confidence and self-esteem, children also develop a sense of independence. Moreover, helping them learn new skills allows them to be more responsible in the future. If they learn to cook, they are more likely to help you prepare a meal. If they can do their household chores, they will feel proud and more confident about their abilities.

- **Social Skills**

Developing social skills is an important part of child development. It enables a child to develop healthy interpersonal relationships and function within their community. These skills include good manners, communicating with others, and expressing one's needs. There are many different strategies for helping a child develop these skills at various stages of their development.

One way is through play. Pretend play is a great way to develop social skills in kids. It is a low-risk environment where kids can try out new social behaviors without hurting the toy. Children often pretend to be different characters. They can practice their social skills by playing pretend and learning new rules.

Another social skill that children can learn is sportsmanship. While it may seem a simple lesson, good sportsmanship is incredibly important because kids have ample opportunities to behave in a positive, healthy manner, both on the field of play and off of it.

Social skills activities build on one another as the child ages, so investing the time to teach good character ideals.

- **Other Skills**

Problem-solving skill training is a great way to help your child grow into adulthood. For example, you can teach them how to run a washing machine or direct GPS. Similarly, you can engage your children in activities that will help them develop their emotional intelligence. For example, they can learn to work in a team and be patient. They can also learn to be empathic by reading stories about others.

Another skill that can be taught to children is self-control, one of the most important soft skills. Children need to know when to say "no." It is also important for them to learn how to share. You can involve your children in play dates or join local parenting groups. Children will eventually learn that it is okay to share even if they do not like it at first.

Children Can Learn at an Early Age

Teaching children social skills early on has many benefits. You can help them develop a wide variety of skills, including self-care. Children can learn to care for themselves using an alarm clock, laying out their hairbrush and toothbrush, and choosing appropriate clothing for the next day's activities. Use visuals to explain this process to your children. Create daily flashcards with pictures that show the process and give them a visual reminder of what needs to be done.

Another important parenting skill is modeling adaptability. This skill will help your child learn that things often differ from what they expected. It will also help them understand that life is an adventure. Things will change, and they will break their plans. However, this is all part of the fun.

Strengthening Parent-Child Relationships

If you are looking for ways of strengthening parent-child relationships, there are several techniques you can use. These include active listening, respecting your child's opinions and feelings, and spending quality time with them. Another technique is conflict resolution, which will require you to discuss the issues with your child so that you can reach a mutually beneficial agreement.

- **Active Listening**

Active listening is a powerful communication tool that you can use to build stronger parent-child relationships. It helps to create a deeper understanding of the other person and allows you to respond better to non-verbal communication. Active listeners notice non-verbal cues, while passive listeners ignore them. Active listening helps you to pick up on a person's feelings and intentions without interrupting them.

Active listening can strengthen parent-child relationships by allowing children to express their feelings and process problems more effectively. It also helps children to develop a healthy self-image. A child will feel valued and loved when their parents listen to what they have to say.

- **Showing Respect for Your Child's Feelings and Opinions**

Showing respect for your child's feelings, thoughts, and values is vital to establishing a positive parent-child relationship. One of the most important ways is to listen to your child. Ask questions to learn about their interests, feelings, and behavior, and respond appropriately.

While parents often feel that their children should respect them, it is important to remember that respect must be reciprocal. You must be able to listen to your child's concerns, acknowledge their individuality, and set clear expectations. It is also important to give your child guidance when they fail to meet these expectations.

- **Spending Quality Time With Your Child**

Spending quality time with your child is a wonderful way to strengthen parent-child relationships. One of the most important is simply focusing your attention on your child.

- **Conflict Resolution**

The management of parent-child conflict varies between cultures due to cultural norms. The concepts of individualism and collectivism may oversimplify the differences, as individuals within society differ in many ways. For example, in the United States, families highly value nonconfrontation in conflict and tend toward collectivist communication behaviors.

Parents can help their children improve their conflict resolution skills by teaching them how to deal with conflict. Children learn by observing their parents. As a result, the use of conflict resolution can improve parent-child relationships. Research has shown that if parents can learn how to manage conflict, they are more likely to help their children develop more resilient relationships.

Parents must model reflective listening and perspective-taking during a conflict. When a child expresses frustration or anger, the parent should reflect on what the child says. The parent should also demonstrate how to negotiate and make a compromise. The child will gain respect when the parent reflects on this behavior.

Once the connection has been restored, discussing solutions is much easier. A child may be unable to use logical thinking if they are still operating on emotion. It might be necessary to ask your child to describe how things could have been better if they had used logic.

Chapter 7:
Basic Rules for Successful Co-Parenting

Co-parenting is a parenting arrangement used after a divorce in which both parents continue to take part in the upbringing and activities of their children. There will be a lot of parent-child contact in this (both in public and private). Co-parenting with a narcissist can be incredibly challenging.

In a co-parenting relationship, both parents have equal responsibilities for the child or children. Unlike a romantic relationship, this relationship focuses entirely on the child and the child's needs. Creating a routine is essential to co-parenting. In addition, it is important to communicate with your ex and establish ground rules for the child's life.

- **Creating a Routine**

The parents work together to provide stability and consistency for their children, including making joint decisions about when the child should go to bed and spending holiday time together. The parents also communicate openly about their goals for the child. Children will adjust to the changes without feeling neglected or ignored.

The schedules of the two parents should be the same, so they can easily communicate. Children also benefit from a predictable schedule, which is especially important when school schedules are involved. It is also helpful to let the school know about the co-parenting situation so they can readily access the parent's contact information. Separate copies of school materials can also be sent to each parent, making communication between the parents much easier.

- **Creating Ground Rules**

Setting ground rules is an important part of creating a co-parenting relationship. This way, both parties will know what is expected of them. It will also protect the children. Rules help make relationships safe. Without rules, parents cannot feel safe with each other, and children cannot feel safe in their families. The co-parent should be supportive in helping the other parent create ground rules that are mutually acceptable to each other.

Another important ground rule is to ensure that the co-parents spend quality time with the child. That means that parents must communicate effectively to ensure they do not interrupt one another's time with their child.

- **Communicating With Your Co-Parent**

Communication with your co-parent is a vitally important part of parenting your child. When it comes to co-parenting, you want to do everything to make the process as smooth as possible. When parents fail to communicate with each other, negative emotions often arise. Instead of focusing on what the other party did wrong, use language to concentrate on solutions to the problem.

Effective co-parenting communication is important to a harmonious outcome. The key is to maintain a professional, child-focused approach to communication. You can accomplish this by treating your ex like a colleague, being respectful and cordial, and maintaining a consistent tone. You should avoid focusing on the former partner's needs and keep the conversation focused on the children.

Communicating with your ex requires maturity, which begins by being attentive and listening to your ex's concerns so that you can make the best decisions for your child. It would be best to show restraint when speaking to your ex, as this will prevent you from overreacting. Eventually, you will become so used to your ex's triggers that you will not react as much.

Keep your schedules consistent and communicate effectively. You must be equally responsive to your child's needs and wants. Even when conflicts arise, try to keep your conversations constructive and honest. It may be difficult at first, but once you can communicate effectively, you will find that co-parenting will be much easier.

- **Reaching a Consensus With Your Co-Parent**

When communicating with your co-parent, it is important to be clear and concise to avoid misinterpretation and conflict. It is better to use a professional tone of voice rather than yelling. It will also allow for effective communication.

Avoid using children as messengers. This may cause the children to take sides or get information mixed up. Choose a method of communication that is comfortable for both of you.

- **Avoiding Toxic Co-Parenting**

There are several steps to avoid toxic co-parenting :

Create a parenting plan and stick to it. A parenting plan is a way of setting expectations and keeping everyone on track.

Work with a court-appointed mediator to navigate through and document any issues you encounter. Toxic co-parenting harms children and you should take measures to keep the children safe.

Do not unilaterally make drastic changes. For example, a vegetarian parent should not change their diet and switch to a meat-eating diet unilaterally. It is better to consult an attorney before making drastic changes because you do not want to be accused of bad co-parenting.

- **Have a Specific Communication Plan for Co-Parenting With a Narcissist**

A parenting plan for co-parenting with narcissists should include specific guidelines for communication between parents. In addition, it should consist of shared child-rearing procedures, including rules about discipline, bedtimes, curfews, and religious upbringing.

Setting up a parenting plan is essential to avoiding conflict and minimizing contact between the two parents. Parents should also create a shared calendar to know when each other has parenting time. If the schedules are different, the parties should communicate in writing.

- **Creating a Parenting Plan**

A parenting plan will help ensure your child's safety and well-being if you are co-parenting. It will also help establish the rules of how each parent communicates with the other parent. While writing a parenting plan can be a long process, it will help you avoid confusion by identifying the issues you have to discuss. This exercise will also help you think about your strengths and weaknesses and how they relate to the parenting of your child. It will help you decide how to communicate and resolve any possible disagreements.

After determining the number of visits each parent will have with the child, you should select the best time for each parent to have the child. This schedule should be based on the distance between the parents and how frequently they exchange the child. The goal is to allow both parents equal time with the child.

When co-parenting with a narcissist, it is important to have specific boundaries to control conflict and keep it to a minimum. Setting clear call and visitation schedules is a must. Narcissistic parents will use every means possible to connect with their children. Creating a specific phone call and text message plan can help keep the conflict at bay.

While having a parenting plan can be helpful for all divorced parents, it is especially important when co-parenting with a narcissist. Try to limit the amount of communication to a minimum and allow yourself time to think about what to say before responding.

It is also important to remember that fighting with a narcissist is never in your child's best interest. The more you and your ex can communicate and work together, the better off your child will be.

- **Boundary Overstepping**

Boundary overstepping is one of the most common problems when co-parenting with a narcissist. It can come in many forms. From rude insults in the car to haranguing you at the doctor's office to constant emails or texts containing nasty threats, it can be difficult to establish and maintain healthy boundaries with a narcissist. The best way to overcome this problem is to develop your boundaries early on.

Boundary setting is a process that takes time and practice. If you have been in unhealthy relationships with narcissists, you will likely feel uncomfortable setting boundaries. But it is essential to practice self-compassion when setting boundaries. Ultimately, boundary-setting is about protecting yourself and your family, not imposing your wishes on another person.

While narcissists will always tell you they will change, you should be aware of their erratic, hostile, and explosive behavior. Make sure you document these episodes as thoroughly as possible. In some cases, they will even act as witnesses to help you prove their point.

You should try to avoid phone or face-to-face contact with your narcissistic partner. Try to keep communication with them to email and limit phone calls to issues about your children. If the argument gets too heated, take the child out of the room, and direct the conversation to another activity. Keep in mind that narcissists may still call you, even when you are at work. If you cannot avoid this, you can always try to redirect the calls to email to avoid conflicts.

How to Navigate Co-Parenting

There are some key things to remember while co-parenting. First, make sure you communicate and maintain boundaries. This is especially important to avoid burdening your kids with conflict. Second, be happy and stay positive. You must remain comfortable and healthy to be a good role model for your children.

- **Communication**

Effective communication is key to co-parenting. It reduces the possibility of misunderstandings, conflict, and information loss. It also helps keep communication brief and to the point. Here are some guidelines to help you make sure you are communicating effectively with your co-parent.

- Agree on a standard report after the child's visitation.
- Stay away from swearing or rude language.
- Agree on a method for quick updates in case of emergencies.

- Speak with respect and civility: When communicating with your co-parent, act as if you are communicating with a colleague. Avoid badmouthing your co-parent in front of the children. Always remember that the child's welfare comes first. If your co-parent is not a good influence, do not talk negatively about them in front of the child.
- Avoid arguing: Arguments are rarely resolved through communication. Instead of arguing, parents should agree to solve the issue in the best way possible. They should seek mediation if a conflict cannot be settled through negotiation. Mediation is a great option despite the difficulties involved if you cannot agree on an issue.

- **Avoiding Burdening Your Children With Conflict**

If you are co-parenting with another parent, it is important to avoid burdening your children with conflict. Even though disagreements are natural and common in all relationships, they can harm your kids' well-being. To avoid burdening your kids with conflict, follow some simple guidelines:

First, avoid putting your kids in the middle of your conflict. It is not helpful for your child to be forced to choose sides when experiencing many changes. Instead, work through your dispute in a way that does not put the child in the middle.

Second, you should focus on the long-term picture. Children deserve to have a good relationship with both parents and extended family. If you are worried that your ex is burdening your children with conflict, identify the issues and discuss them with your ex. Once you have identified the problem, re-define your expectations for supporting extended family relationships.

- **Keeping Yourself Happy**

Co-parenting can be difficult, but there are ways to stay happy and positive while sharing parenting responsibilities with your ex. First, remember to take time for yourself. Self-care may seem impossible or unimportant in the early days of separation or divorce. However, it is important to remember that you are worth your time and energy, and so do your children.

Another way to stay upbeat is to do fun activities when your child is with the other parent. It helps if your child knows you have a life outside them. It also gives them the idea that you are happy. Moreover, children like to see their parents happy. As such, highlighting the positive qualities of each parent will help the children to feel safe.

When co-parenting, it is crucial to maintain consistency in behavior and parenting decisions. Children thrive in an environment where both parents act consistently. It is important to establish basic rules of behavior and enforce them. Also, parents should avoid competing for their children's love. Competing for a child's affection will only cause the children to become unstable.

- **Gray Rocking**

When you are co-parenting with a narcissist, the best way to protect your children is to avoid engaging in arguments. Narcissists will try to bait you into arguments, so it is crucial to resist the temptation.

One of the best ways to do this is to use the gray rock method. This technique involves a polite way of refusing to engage. Choose to be uninteresting. Choose not to do battle with the narcissist. In doing so, the narcissist will lose interest in you because it is no longer fun for them.

Plus, you will avoid alienating them and will also avoid causing harm to your children.

Gray rocking is not a long-term strategy. It should be used for a few brief breaks, not as a constant pattern. If you repeat this tactic too often, your narcissistic ex may become frustrated.

Chapter 8:
Establishing Co-Parenting Goals

When a relationship is dissolved, if a child is involved, special care needs to be made to ensure that the child is cared for. Despite any animosity one parent may feel for another, they must work together for their child.

Co-Parenting Goals

It is important to establish co-parenting goals to help both parents develop a common goal and will help clarify their responsibilities in parenting decisions. Ideally, parents will share joint decision-making power over major issues such as discipline and medical care.

Parents want their children to be happy and have strong relationships. However, when parents find themselves in a challenging situation, they often use their energy in ways that are not productive or go against their desired outcomes. The challenges of co-parenting often cause parents to become emotionally reactive and act irrationally.

Setting co-parenting goals is a positive start to re-establishing a relationship. It will help you to create a consistent routine and rules for your children. You should also take the time to complement each other, if possible.

Tips for Setting Co-Parenting Guidelines

If you and your co-parent have agreed to share the custody of your children, setting co-parenting guidelines is an important step. These guidelines help to keep your communications focused and limit opportunities for conflict. Make sure your co-parent knows what is expected of them and how to communicate with them constructively.

- **Communication With Co-Parents**

One of the first things to consider when setting up co-parenting guidelines is communication. In all relationships, communication is the key to success. Communication is the process of conveying information and is effective if both the sender and the receiver understand what is being said. There are many types of communication, including verbal and nonverbal. Both parties must receive and understand the message in all cases.

Although it may be difficult to be unbiased, your communications with your co-parent should be professional and focused on your children's best interests. Keeping your contacts focused on your child's needs will keep things professional and peaceful and help you work toward your goals.

Communication should occur as often as possible. If possible, set up a schedule for communication with your co-parent. It is also important to set caveats for big decisions, deadlines, and emergencies. Once you have established a schedule, communicate with your co-parent frequently. Also, update each other as new information about your child comes to light.

It is vital to remember that you and your co-parent will have disagreements about how to handle situations that arise. Although discord is inevitable, respecting each other will go a long way toward a satisfactory outcome. Be considerate of your ex's needs and opinions by notifying them of upcoming events, informing them of your child's activities at school, and taking their views seriously. If you do not agree, try to work through the disagreements privately rather than involving the children. If you cannot resolve your disputes this way, you may have to contact a third party for assistance.

- **Creating a Parenting Plan With Your Ex**

It is important to remember that the parenting plan you create with your ex should be based on what is best for the children, and both parents should make sacrifices. Sometimes, your partner may not realize that you are making compromises. But that is okay. After all, it is only natural to want what is best for your kids.

If you have legitimate concerns about your ex's parenting style, make sure you put those concerns in writing. Remember that these concerns are different from concerns about drug use. It is important not to put the children in the middle of your divorce or the resulting custody battles. Instead, try to reassure your children of your love and support for them and spend quality time with them.

Assuming you can agree on a parenting plan, you must ensure it is compatible with your child's activities. For example, you must consider pick-ups at school or sports practice. If you are splitting time with your ex, you will also need to consider their schedule. In a parenting plan, your child's needs must always come first.

- **Creating a Parenting Schedule With Your Ex**

If you and your ex have children together, creating a parenting schedule is a great way to help the kids adjust to divorce. It shows the kids that both parents are willing to work together and meet the needs of the children. Developing a parenting schedule involves balancing logistics and your commitments to the children.

The first step is to put aside your differences and devise a schedule that will work for everyone. It should be fair for the children and will give both parents equal time with them. A standard custody agreement may be necessary if you and your ex cannot reach a mutually agreeable schedule. This agreement will give the non-custodial parent one evening a week and every other weekend.

Once you have established a schedule, you must check in with your ex at least once a year. You can use this time to suggest ideas and make changes as necessary. However, it is important to note that you can only change the schedule if both parents agree.

- **Avoiding Toxic Co-Parents**

Setting co-parenting guidelines is crucial for parents who want to ensure consistency and avoid toxic co-parents. The procedures must be clear and contain provisions for communication, punishment and rewards, calendar and scheduling, medical care, and financials. The agreement should also spell out how to deal with disagreements.

Toxic fighting between co-parents is especially harmful to the health of their children. It can lower the child's cognitive performance and even cause physical illnesses. It can also increase the risk of substance abuse and eating disorders. Therefore, both parents should agree not to disparage the other in front of children. Additionally, parents should not allow their children to talk disrespectfully about their siblings or parents.

When setting co-parenting guidelines, keep communication short and to the point. Avoid discussing things that do not directly affect your children or discussing artificially concerning things. Avoid escalating conflict by sticking to the facts when communicating with your ex. If your ex becomes defensive or sarcastic, it is best to limit your communication.

Chapter 9:
Effective Co-Parenting Strategies

Effective co-parenting is a challenge that requires maturity and the ability to set aside egos. Parents must work together to provide their children with the same level of stability, safety, and consistency they want. Children are looking for a united front. They must feel that both parents are committed to their children's best interests.

- **Respect Each Other**

Co-parenting partners need to respect each other and make sure they communicate promptly. It is important to communicate professionally and not withhold details that may affect the children. This will reduce ambiguity in communications and prevent conflict. Whether you live together or apart, co-parenting is a long-term commitment to your child, and you must treat each other with respect and cooperation.

As co-parents, it is normal to have disagreements over certain issues. Taking the time to be civil will show your children that they come first. It will also model maturity to the children. Instead of expressing your frustrations and anger, consider discussing it with a friend or therapist. Your children do not deserve to carry the burden of your ill feelings, and venting too much can damage their relationship with the other parent.

- **Avoid Negative Comments**

During co-parenting, one of the biggest challenges is avoiding negative comments. These can hurt the other parent and affect the children, so it is important to avoid making them. Negative comments are a common form of anger directed at the other parent. The child may not realize it, but they absorb these comments and internalize them.

If your co-parent makes negative comments, avoid directly arguing with them. An argument only reinforces the negative energy in the situation, so it is best to keep your mouth shut. Instead, wait until the negative energy has dissipated. This can take minutes or even days. Stopping the conflict prevents it from intensifying and shows your co-parent that you are willing to change your behavior.

- **Put Children's Needs First**

When co-parenting, it is important to put your children's needs first to ensure their happiness and overall health. Both parents must communicate with the children to know they can depend on them. If you and your spouse have different parenting styles, let that go and focus on what is best for your child. It may mean compromising with your spouse sometimes, but protecting your child's best interests is necessary.

The first step towards a successful co-parenting relationship is creating a support system. This can include a close friend or a trusted religious leader.

- **Avoid Blaming the Other Parent**

Avoid blame-based communication if you disagree with the other parent about parenting issues. A blame style of communication can lead to counter-blame and defensiveness. Instead, work together to address the problems from a common point of view. You can also document your child's behavior.

During meetings with your ex, avoid using sarcastic or offensive language. Be polite and respectful to the other parent. Avoid addressing the other parent as a "loser" or "greedy b****." Such statements will not go over well. Similarly, avoid using false formalities in email exchanges. False pleasantries may come across as sarcastic.

- **Avoid Laying a Lonely Guilt Trip on Your Ex**

When communicating with your ex during co-parenting, it is important to remain mature and avoid laying a lonely guilt trip. While offering an apology for any transgression is perfectly acceptable, it is important to be brief, sincere, and move on. You know your ex well enough to recognize their triggers. While pushing your ex away and being aggressive is easy, this does not solve the problem.

Avoid using abusive language. Abusing language can come across as bitter and threatening. Instead, use classy language and consider your voice's tone before speaking. You can also mentally play out your responses before speaking. You will have more opportunities to communicate your point of view if you do not overreact to every little thing.

- **Create a Co-Parenting Plan Early in the Divorce Process**

Creating a co-parenting plan is important to protect your children during the divorce. This plan should be specific, and parents should collaborate to devise the best strategy for their children. A good parenting plan will avoid disagreements about parenting time or other issues.

Both parents need to make sacrifices for the benefit of the children, especially if they have children of school age. For example, traveling between two homes is not ideal for a school-age child, so it is important to figure out how to give them both parents.

Three Ways to Resolve Co-Parenting Conflict

The first step is to talk to your ex about the issues. You may not want to deal with the issue second-hand if you have kids, so try to speak directly with your ex. Choose a neutral location where you can talk about the conflict without the children present.

- **Avoid the Blame Game**

When parents argue, it is often easy to blame the other parent. This is especially true if the co-parent is toxic, as this type of parent does not take responsibility for their actions. In addition, they do not reflect on their behavior to understand where they can improve. These parents often trash the other parent in front of the kids. They may even use the children to make their ex look bad. This type of parent may think they are protecting the children or trying to avoid having the kids like them.

While constructive feedback can be valuable, it is best to avoid placing blame on co-parenting conflict. This tactic is unhelpful and has no place in a healthy relationship. However, it is important to recognize when an issue is worth fighting over. If it is, then you need to know how to fight smart.

In addition to avoiding placing blame, co-parents should also try to find cooperative solutions to their conflict. Instead of using it as an opportunity to assign blame, parents should view it as an opportunity to improve their relationship. Blaming is unproductive and rarely results in any constructive momentum for repairing the problem.

Another strategy for preventing co-parenting conflict is apologizing. This tactic works best when both parties admit that they made a mistake. Apologizing for mistakes or wrongdoing immediately can prevent a conflict from escalating.

- **Avoid Accusations**

The best way to resolve co-parenting conflict is to avoid accusations and keep the children out of the mix. Sometimes it will be necessary to confront your ex to resolve issues, and avoiding accusations will ensure the kids are safe and your relationship with them stays positive.

While it is understandable to feel frustrated and resentful sometimes, it is important to avoid blaming your ex for the problems. Instead, you should try to talk honestly about the issues causing conflict.

Acknowledge your partner's concerns and suggest ways to solve the conflict. This tactic can help clarify your perception of the problem, which is often the key to resolving the conflict. By doing this, you can begin the healing process. Acknowledging your partner's concerns will help you avoid escalating conflict and build trust.

If your ex is using abusive methods of discipline against you and your children, talk to your ex about it. If the situation is urgent, call 911 or contact a lawyer. But if the problem is not life-threatening, consider discussing the matter in a non-judgmental manner.

Focus on the parenting styles and attitudes of each other. A common problem is a lack of empathy. You should encourage your ex to see the other side of the situation with compassion and empathy. If you cannot agree on what to do, you can still make the child feel better.

- **Focus on the Child's Needs**

Several techniques can improve the situation if there is a co-parenting conflict. First, consider your child's needs. This may mean focusing on your child's needs during the conversation. Children may learn to imitate their parents' and peers' behaviors, so it is important to remember that a child may be watching how you act or talk to them. Secondly, try to avoid bringing your emotional issues into the conversation.

It would be best if you always put your child's needs before yours as a parent. You can focus on your child's needs and wishes in the conversation and reach a mutually beneficial solution. Moreover, you will be able to get your child back more quickly if you do not have to keep arguing for hours and days.

Another useful strategy for resolving co-parenting conflict is to use social-psychological problem-solving. This method helps parents move from a personal relationship to a professional one. It incorporates conflict-resolution skills training as well as co-parenting education. However, it is not the same as parenting classes, as this method is more holistic and child-centered.

Effective communication is key to creating a supportive co-parenting relationship. Ensure you communicate clearly and concisely and avoid hurting your ex's feelings. As parents, it is important to respect each other's feelings and try to see the world from your child's perspective. Focus on your child's needs and the needs of their extended family, and re-defining your expectations.

Chapter 10:
How to Co-Parent Without Arguing

Maintaining a cordial relationship with your ex-spouse can be difficult, but you can co-parent without arguing and maintain your relationship with your kids. To co-parent successfully, you should establish ground rules, maintain boundaries, and show compassion toward each other. While it can be challenging, remember that your children are your priority.

- **Setting Ground Rules**

One of the easiest ways to avoid co-parenting arguing is to set clear ground rules for communication. One good example is to reply to each other's messages within 24 hours. If you cannot respond within that time frame, you can ask the other parent to clarify. Setting these ground rules will ensure that both parents win in the end.

As parents, you are responsible for spending quality time with your children and should not interfere with the other parent's time with your children. For instance, you should not call them constantly during their time with their child. Instead, agree on the major issues that will affect your children.

- **Keeping Up With Your Kids**

The first step in co-parenting without arguing with your kids is to respect one another's parenting style. Children need both parents to be active in their lives and to show interest in their lives. It is also important to have the same rules and routines, such as the same curfew, similar methods of discipline, and similar routines of making meals and paying attention to their schoolwork. You can also avoid arguing with your kids directly if you set up channels of communication.

The next step in co-parenting without arguing with your kids is to be realistic. Remember that your arguments before the separation will not be relevant to your relationship with your children. Instead, you need to focus on raising your children together.

- **Maintaining Boundaries**

Creating co-parenting boundaries is essential for a healthy relationship. The limits should reflect the impact each person has on the co-parenting relationship. By setting boundaries in advance, you will be able to set realistic expectations for yourself and your partner. This can prevent unnecessary arguments and frustrations.

The most important part of setting boundaries when co-parenting is ensuring your children have two parents and a healthy relationship with both. Setting boundaries and communicating them is essential to creating a happy, healthy, stable family life for your kids. But it is also crucial not to get too personal - this will only invite conflict and make communication difficult. It is also a good idea to separate your personal life from your children's. That way, your ex will not get as involved in your child's upbringing as you do.

Setting boundaries and focusing on the children's needs should be your focus. During co-parenting, remember that you are not friends with your ex and that the children are the most important thing. You may still want to maintain a friendship, but it is a bad idea to talk about issues in your relationship when your children are around. In addition to setting boundaries, you should try communicating with your ex as if you were co-workers.

- **Compassion**

Some parents may have difficulty co-parenting after divorce. While some may be friendly, others may find it impossible to spend time together without arguing. The key is to be calm and keep a professional demeanor. Avoid making demands or discussing past conflicts with your former partner. You can foster trust and move forward as collaborative co-parents by avoiding these behaviors.

Communication is critical whether you are co-parenting for the first time or have been married for years. Pick up the phone when they are available and respond to texts promptly. If you both maintain respectful communication, your kids will pick up on that.

- **Positive Reinforcement**

Positive reinforcement is an effective way to improve your relationship with your children without arguing. It builds trust and encourages the child to open up to you and seek advice and support. This method also enables you to accomplish more with less effort. Here are some tips for using positive reinforcement.

Start by recognizing your child's good behavior. This will help prevent tantrums and physical aggression. It will also help to improve your child's communication skills. Children respond better to praise than criticism, so give your child plenty of praise whenever he or she does something good.

Another way to improve co-parenting is to compliment each other's parenting styles. By complimenting each other, the children will see that their parents are worthy of praise. It also helps to follow the rules you and your co-parent have set. Give both parents advance notice of these rules.

Chapter 11:
Co-Parenting with a Narcissist Parent

When a child has a narcissistic parent, they must work through their feelings. Doing so will help them learn how to have healthy relationships and overcome negative feelings left behind by narcissistic parents. Several things can help:

- **Encourage Healthy Narcissism in Children**

Children with narcissistic parents are more likely to develop low self-esteem because they never feel special and celebrated for who they are. They are also more likely to feel neglected and devalued.

When dealing with a narcissistic parent, setting boundaries is essential to protect both co-parents and children from emotional damage. In addition, it also helps to document discipline protocols, schedules, and extracurricular activities for the children. The documentation can support the parent when the narcissist tries to shift blame. It will also help mitigate the inevitable fights.

Written guidelines will make the narcissistic parent accountable.

- **Avoid Gaslighting**

When we hear things often enough, we begin to suspect that what we thought to be true is not. If you suspect that a narcissistic parent is gaslighting you or your child, there are ways to protect yourself from this manipulative behavior.

First, find a support network for you and your child. Some other adults and children have similar experiences and may be able to offer suggestions on managing feelings.

Talk with an unbiased counselor. This person's neutral perspective will keep you both grounded in the truth.

It is also helpful to write down your feelings. If you suspect that a parent is gaslighting you, document the interactions. Journaling will help you verify your memories and experiences and protect you from manipulation. It is also a good idea to cut off contact with the manipulative parent.

- **Avoid Comparisons**

If you are dealing with a narcissistic parent, it is critical to avoid comparisons. This is because the narcissistic parent will likely make needless comparisons and disparaging comments.

This kind of behavior will lead to a child feeling pressured to be the perfect son or daughter and to live life according to the expectations of the narcissistic parent. However, you must help your child understand that he or she cannot live up to every parent's wish.

Narcissistic parents often compare their children to their peers and siblings in an attempt to control an out-of-control world. It can also be an attempt to get their children to fight for attention or feel less than others. In other words, narcissistic parents try to control the world they perceive as out of control.

- **Avoid Blaming**

The best way to deal with a narcissistic parent is to avoid blaming them. These parents will often try to make you feel inferior and small.

They may also use triangulation to justify their actions. This tactic can make things worse rather than better.

Another tactic to avoid blaming is to minimize your contact with the narcissistic parent. They will likely give up on you if you do not respond to their demands. By not showing emotion or concern for them, you will be able to sabotage their abusive behavior and save yourself from further abuse.

- **Release Anger**

Narcissists cannot use cognitive judgment when they are in a fit of rage, so their behavior can be out of control. When confronted by a narcissist, do not try to argue with them; instead, ask them to stop by walking away or wait until the next day. You will be able to remain calm and avoid further confrontation.

There are healthy ways to relieve your anger. Physical activity, venting, or even crying can all help you release your feelings. Releasing anger is a necessary emotional response after you have identified the abuse. It is natural to feel angry because you feel like you have been wronged or did not realize it sooner.

Narcissistic Triangulation – How Do Narcissists Treat Their Adult Children?

Adult children of narcissists are often left with childhood trauma because narcissists tend to blame their bad behavior on their children. Narcissists also fail to set clear boundaries with their adult children.

- **Narcissists Fail to Empathize With Their Children**

Narcissists fail to empathize with their adult children in several ways. This includes not validating their children's feelings or using gaslighting to avoid admitting mistakes. They rarely own up to their actions or inactions.

Narcissists have a unique way of projecting their problems onto others. They deny the bad aspects of themselves and punish those who hurt them. For example, a narcissistic mother will project an unreal image of herself onto her adult children.

- **Narcissists May Triangulate**

The impact of narcissistic triangulation can be devastating to all involved, but there are ways to navigate it. Although it can be tricky, setting personal boundaries and seeking support outside the narcissist's circle is essential to navigating narcissistic behavior.

Often, narcissists will use their children as bait to sway other members of their family. This tactic is an effort to maintain control over the family, as children of narcissists will constantly try to gain the approval of their parents. They may also threaten the child when they try to distance themselves.

- **Narcissists Blame Their Bad Behavior on Their Children**

The adult children of a narcissist rarely have autonomy. They must rely on the narcissist, who does not take responsibility for their behavior and does not allow their children to develop a sense of self. This narcissistic behavior carries over into adulthood and creates a cycle of self-blame.

- **Narcissists Do Not Set Boundaries With Their Adult Children**

Even though this type of personality disorder is not easy to deal with, the good news is that it is possible to learn how to set boundaries with a narcissist. To start, set clear limits and communicate them effectively. Remember that boundaries are personal, not universal.

- **Narcissists May Engage in 'Scapegoating'**

One sign that the adult children of a narcissist are engaging in scapegoating is the victim's altered self-image. The adult child's distorted self-image can cause that person to distrust others and lead to excessive self-criticism. Often, an adult child of a narcissist may find themselves attracted to controlling or narcissistic partners. Unfortunately, there is no recognized condition for this syndrome, so it is often assumed to be a side effect of being the golden child.

As a result, scapegoating can become a very powerful weapon in the hands of a narcissist. The scapegoat is a victim of decades of abuse by a narcissist. Once exposed, the scapegoat has been forced to enter survival mode. To maintain the family's relationship with the scapegoat, the child learns to adopt a compliant persona and suppress any signs of dissatisfaction.

- **Narcissists May Engage in 'Invisible Child'**

'Invisible child' syndrome is a form of child abuse in which the child feels like an 'invisible' person. As a result, they become very independent and often feel unloved and unworthy. Because of these issues, they are highly susceptible to severe depression and may even engage in unhealthy behaviors.

- **Narcissists May Engage in 'Golden Child'**

Adult children of narcissists often exhibit the characteristics of a 'golden child.' They lack emotional sensitivity and struggle to establish meaningful connections with others. They are also comfortable manipulating others for their benefit. They are often molded into mini-me versions of their parents and given the most attention.

Golden children are usually hypersensitive to criticism and are obsessed with perfection. They expect everything to be perfect, from their clothes to their rooms. They also expect their homework to be error-free and without mistakes. These high expectations can have a lasting impact on their behavior.

How to Help Your Children Emotionally Detach From a Narcissistic Parent

It is often difficult for adult children of narcissistic parents to detach emotionally from them. It can be difficult to let go of the old habit of trying to please their parent, especially if that parent is manipulative.

But you can help the children learn to detach from this habit by first acknowledging the pain they are experiencing. It is important to understand that acknowledging their psychic pain does not mean that they should relive that pain or anguish. Accepting their pain will make it easier to detach emotionally from their parent.

While it may be tempting to confront a narcissist, they should be aware that this rarely offers relief. The narcissist will try to control them and sabotage their internal self-worth. It would be best if they remained calm and did not respond to the narcissist's criticisms or insults.

Narcissists often threaten their children with physical harm or even emotional cutoff if they fail to meet expectations. This type of narcissism can make children ashamed of their feelings, and they must take responsibility for them.

Emotionally detaching from a narcissistic parent is not easy, but it is a necessary step for the children's well-being. If they can do it, they will be able to build a strong foundation of peace and hope for the future.

Dealing With Toxic Shame

This emotional state is a natural response to being raised in a world of narcissism. It results from being forced to conform to a narcissistic parent's demands and expectations. In this environment, the instinct is to make oneself small and hide from the world. The result is a cycle of shame.

Toxic shame can make it difficult for a child to deal with narcissistic parents. This parent will often try to manipulate the child by blaming them for what they do or buy. They may also talk badly about their children to other family members or attempt to convince their children that they are the problem. This kind of parenting can lead to children's self-abandonment or even self-harm.

Narcissistic parents are notoriously critical of children and only notice their child when it suits them. Because narcissistic parents rarely give encouraging words to their children, they become self-conscious adults.

Narcissistic parents' toxic behavior is exhausting and can result in long-term emotional issues. Their lack of insight and manipulation makes it impossible for their children to develop trust in them. Because of this, children may become emotionally unstable and suffer from emotional flashbacks.

Chapter 12:
Set Boundaries When Co-Parenting With a Narcissist

If your ex had narcissistic tendencies in your marriage, it will definitely manifest in how they manage their parental responsibilities. Dealing with your narcissistic ex after your divorce is one thing, but being compelled to do so because you are parenting children together is quite another.

When co-parenting with someone who is a narcissist, it is critical to set clear boundaries. Narcissists crave control and may try to manipulate you into saying or doing things you would not normally say or do. Their tactics include pressure and exploitation of your children. The best way to avoid a narcissist is to limit contact with them or avoid any contact altogether. Narcissists feed off your children's details, and they may use the children to manipulate you.

The narcissist will likely resist the boundaries you put into place. Besides creating clear boundaries, you should also create a solid parenting plan. Make sure to document everything so you have proof of your dealings.

It is not easy being a parent. Parenting together with a narcissist makes it even more challenging. While co-parenting with a narcissist can be difficult, setting up clear boundaries with them can help you feel more at ease, protect your child, and make handling the situation easier.

Here are some boundaries you can put in place to keep both you and your children safe:

- **Avoiding Bad-Mouthing**

Avoiding bad-mouthing when co-parenting with a narcissist is a critical aspect of co-parenting. Children do not like it when one or both parents speak ill of the other. They do not want to be put in a position of taking sides and want to feel that both parents love them. However, this behavior undermines a healthy parent-child relationship.

The best way to avoid bad-mouthing is to avoid engaging in it yourself. Bad-mouthing is detrimental not only to you but also to your children. As a parent, you are the role model for your children, and it is your job to keep them safe.

Narcissists often use their children as pawns, bringing them into a fight to gain their advantage. When this happens, it is important to tell your child that this behavior is unacceptable and to stay away. Your child needs to see you standing up for them. Take your child somewhere else or to a play area but avoid letting them witness a fight.

- **Children as Pawns**

You should never allow your narcissistic co-parent to use your children as pawns and should use action-based consequences to prevent this behavior. It is also important to remember that your narcissistic co-parent enjoys chaos and can be emotionally exhausting.

If your narcissist can manipulate your children to achieve their goals, it is essential to document these behaviors. You can use evidence to support your story if they use the children to win the custody battle. Hiring an attorney with experience dealing with narcissists is also wise to protect your children.

Children are incredibly perceptive and often pick up on their parents' behavior. While they may not realize it, they often blame one parent for the conflicts. If your narcissist is using your child as a weapon, you must work to undo the damage they have caused in their lives.

What Must a Co-Parent Refrain From Doing?

While the kids' best interest should always come first, there are several things to avoid while co-parenting, such as competing with your ex and being rigid just for rigidity's sake. Additionally, you must respect each other's time with the kids.

Co-parenting with a narcissist is not easy, and expecting a healthy co-parenting relationship will only lead to frustration and pain. Narcissists need power and self-preservation and live in perpetual anger. They take great pleasure in tormenting others and justifying their wretchedness. It is best to avoid co-parenting with a narcissist if you want your family to remain intact.

In the event of a co-parenting dispute with a narcissist, consider hiring a mediator to help you negotiate your differences. If mediation is not an option, consider having the court order it. But remember, a narcissist will likely not attend the sessions, will devalue the therapist, and will petition for a different therapist.

- **Co-Parents Should Not Compete With Their Ex**

Co-parents should not compete with a former spouse if they still have children. The most important thing to remember is that the children belong to both parents. If you want to co-parent with your ex, you must set boundaries for the children so that neither parent feels a need to be stricter than the other.

- **Co-Parents Should Avoid Rigidity for the Sake of It**

Rigidity is a bad thing in co-parenting. Judges dislike clock-watchers, and rigidity is not acceptable for the sake of rigidity. Judges often look down on co-parents who let their petty grudges get in the way of what is best for the children. Keeping a positive attitude about the other parent's flexibility is vital, and letting the other parent exchange the child or children later is perfectly acceptable.

- **Co-Parents Should Respect Each Other's Time With the Children**

It is also important to appreciate each other's parenting styles. Many co-parents have different parenting styles and do not respect the other parent's time with the children. Doing so will only make the children feel disrespected and hurt.

Chapter 13:
The Challenges of Co-Parenting With a Narcissist

When co-parenting with a narcissistic ex, prepare for the co-parenting experience before you begin. You should also make sure to avoid arguments during co-parenting.

Co-Parenting With a Narcissistic Ex

If your ex is a narcissist, co-parenting with them can be difficult. This personality will try to control your child through manipulation and deceit.

It is very important to avoid face-to-face communication with your ex, as facial expressions and tone of voice can be used against you. Also, avoid talking to your ex in front of your children. If you must meet your ex face-to-face, bring a friend to help you. Set up a communication system where you can communicate with your ex only about your children and finances.

It would be best if you avoided physical contact with them. Limit your contact and communication to emails and keep it to a minimum. If they do try to call you, end the conversation quickly. If you are at work, your ex may still call you, but if they do, make sure you do not respond. Instead, email your response so you can avoid conflicts in the future.

Preparing for Co-Parenting

Co-parenting with your narcissistic ex requires adjustment and change in your ways of dealing with them. Fortunately, there are ways to help make the process easier.

First, you must understand that your ex will not share your values or prioritize your needs over theirs. They will not share parenting responsibilities and will be unlikely to have empathy for those who have been unfairly treated. Consequently, dealing with a narcissist is important for your recovery and your children's well-being.

Establishing boundaries is critical. Narcissists tend to use manipulative tactics and abuse their victims' emotions. To prevent future battles, develop healthy boundaries. For instance, if your ex is a frequent texter, try not to answer their messages. Instead, email your responses to avoid potential conflict.

Avoiding Arguments

Avoiding arguments when co-parenting with your narcissistic ex is an important part of the process. It will help you avoid the worst-case scenario. Since narcissists feed on attention, the best way to avoid disputes is to ignore them.

When possible, limit in-person conversations as they can turn into a conflict in front of your children. Instead, use mail or text messages to communicate with your ex. This gives you space to think and keep your conversations on the topic.

Avoiding disputes while co-parenting with your narcissistic ex can be a challenging task. Even if both parents are generally agreeable, you will still need to set boundaries for your child. You can use many strategies to prevent the onset of arguments and maintain the relationship.

Set up a communication schedule. If you live in the same home as your ex, try to avoid arguments by focusing on the children's needs and interests. Narcissists blame others when things do not go as they believe they should.

Avoid using your children in the cold war. Never use your child to attack your ex or engage in taunting. Do not use your child to vent your anger or spy on your ex. If your child witnesses your fight, they may not understand why you are upset.

Find a support group for narcissistic parents. You can learn how to handle difficult situations by sharing your concerns with others. It is a good idea to seek professional legal advice. These professionals will be able to protect you from being gaslighted and manipulated.

How to Help the Kids With the Narcissistic Games

Narcissists target people-pleasers. They divide and conquer, create jealousy, and triangulate. You can help your children learn right from wrong by establishing boundaries. But it would be best if you never ignored the narcissistic signs.

It is crucial to remember that narcissists play mind games, and children are especially vulnerable to this. You must keep them away from the narcissist to ensure they do not become prey, as children do not know how to protect themselves.

Another tactic narcissists use is guilt. The narcissist will make a person feel bad for leaving them. The narcissist will often blame their failures on the children, which will only further damage their self-esteem.

If you are worried about your children's relationships with a narcissist, there are several things you can do to prevent them from becoming victims. One way is to teach them empathy. Empathy is a skill that can be learned, but too much of it is dangerous because users will abuse the person's innate kindness.

Children of narcissists are often subject to a cycle of idealization and devaluation. They are alternately loved and put down and forced to jump through hoops to please their parent. This cycle is stressful for the children.

One of the most common games a narcissist employs is isolation. Narcissists want to control everyone around them and become the only social support. Their actions can cause people to lose touch with their family members and create problems with others.

Protecting your kids from the narcissist's games is one of the hardest things to deal with in a narcissistic relationship. Narcissists are highly unpredictable. They may say untrue things, manipulate you, and make you feel inferior. Narcissists will also play the victim. They will attempt to deflect responsibility and accountability through emotional stories that may or may not be true.

It is essential to show empathy to your children. This will help prevent them from exhibiting narcissistic behavior as adults. It is possible to teach empathy but remember that too much empathy can make you feel sorry for others and leave you vulnerable to being used by others.

While it is easy to dismiss the effects of narcissistic games, you must take a closer look at how these games affect your child's self-esteem and develop better ways to help them cope with these games. Parents who overvalue their children have a greater chance of them showing narcissistic tendencies.

It can help your child cope with narcissistic games by identifying the narcissist in the environment. Many narcissists like games that emphasize competition and cooperation. Such games reinforce narcissists' traits and are not advisable for kids.

Parents must teach their children self-regulation and be supportive. They should also teach their children that it is okay to make mistakes and to cry after losing. This helps them learn to take responsibility for their actions.

Chapter 14:
Parallel Parenting - A Safer Alternative to Co-Parenting?

Parallel parenting is a form of parenting that allows parents to share custody of their children without requiring cooperative parenting. It can benefit the children, as it shields them from the negative impact of parental conflict. It may be a safer alternative to co-parenting, especially in high-conflict divorces.

Parallel parenting is an option that allows both parents to remain involved in the lives of their children while maintaining some separation. This arrangement can reduce conflict and help families move on from the divorce.

Parents who use parallel parenting prevent their children from becoming the source of parental conflict. However, parallel parenting can be difficult for some couples, particularly if there is deep animosity and stark differences in parenting styles.

If your ex-spouse is a narcissist, you should be particularly cautious. Although your ex-spouse may appear to be a great parent, your children may still be subjected to manipulation and rejection. If you find yourself stuck in this process, limiting contact with your ex-spouse is best. This will help prevent your children from becoming the messenger between two rival parents, which can cause stress and bias.

- **Parallel Parenting Shields Children From the Negative Effects of Parental Conflict**

Parallel parenting is a great co-parenting technique that shields children from the damaging effects of parental conflict. Children exposed to parental conflict are less likely to become good adults. This technique emphasizes that both parents are equally important to the children.

However, it is important to note that this approach is inappropriate for every situation. For example, a couple that exhibits frequent family violence may not be able to handle the parallel parenting arrangement. Conversely, if both parents are committed to co-parenting and the children are willing to accept the plan, parallel parenting may be a viable solution.

One of the benefits of parallel parenting is that it enables both parents to have significant roles in the child's life while still allowing them to maintain a sense of independence and responsibility. Moreover, this parenting approach requires both parents to cooperate on major decisions, which protects the child from the effects of parental conflict.

- **Parallel Parenting Can Be a Safer Alternative to Co-Parenting**

Parents with a checkered past may find parallel parenting a safer alternative to co-parenting. The method emphasizes minimal interaction and adhering to a schedule. It is not recommended for parents to talk on the phone often. Instead, an assigned middle person will coordinate the child's schedule and monitor the level of conflict between the parents.

Parallel parenting shields the child from the conflicts between the two parents. Parents should not air their grievances in front of their children. They should also avoid treating parenting as a competition or comparing styles.

- **Parallel Parenting Can Be a Better Solution for High-Conflict Divorces**

Parallel parenting is a good solution for high-conflict divorces, but it is not perfect. It does not eliminate communication between parents and requires parents to work together to decide the most important matters. These discussions should be collaborative, productive, and center on the children's best interests. However, some parents cannot reach this point quickly or never get there.

Parallel parenting is a good solution for high-conflict divorces if both parents are willing to cooperate and limit their interactions. While it may not be the ideal solution for high-conflict divorces, it does help reduce conflicts between parents and can reduce the need for litigation. Parents can use a third-party facilitator to mediate face-to-face meetings and develop a parenting plan that meets all their needs and expectations.

- **Parallel Parenting Can Give You a Healthy Upbringing for Your Children**

Parallel parenting is an ideal approach for parents in the process of divorce or working out their legal issues. It is also a good option for parents who live far apart and do not communicate much after the divorce. Parallel parenting is not for every parent, however, and may not be suitable if one or both parents have different parenting styles or are inflexible about the process.

Parallel parenting is also a good option for people who find it difficult to co-parent because it puts the children's best interests first. It is also more flexible and will minimize conflict between parents. However, if you and your ex-partner cannot co-parent, you may need to hire a mediator to help you work out the details. This can be arranged through court or other resources, but ultimately, you must decide if it is right for you and your children.

How and When to Use Parallel Parenting

A parallel parenting model may be suitable or inappropriate depending on the parents' relationship. When parents are fighting a lot and there is a chance that one or both of the parents will subject the kids to that conflict, parallel parenting is recommended.

Relationships with a past of inter-partner domestic violence or ones where one parent exhibits narcissistic personality traits are two examples.

However, the scenario changes if this conflict involves or is directed at children. When one parent is abusing the children physically or emotionally, not even parallel parenting is acceptable. Depending on the type and severity of the abuse, the non-abusive spouse should have sole or primary custody (including decision-making).

Should Full Custody Be Considered?

As parents become more adept at handling their differences, they should be able to transition from parallel parenting to co-parenting. Unfortunately, not every couple will succeed in providing their kid with this degree of shared care, and in some situations, full custody may be pursued. You may make the decision to seek full custody of your child if your ex repeatedly violates the terms of the parenting plan, is unable to place your child's needs ahead of their own, or is endangering your child's health or safety.

Be prepared to provide the court with evidence of both your greater ability to parent your kid and of your ex's inability to do so. The determination of whether to grant complete custody frequently depends on the presence of evidence of neglect, narcissistic abuse, a lack of supervision, or substance abuse.

Chapter 15:
The Effects of Narcissistic Abuse on Your Kids

Narcissistic parents often make a lot of demands and requests, and the pressure on the child to comply with them escalates when the child refuses. The child may feel shame or guilt if they do not comply, or the narcissistic parent may threaten them with violence, sabotage, or emotional blackmail.

Signs and Symptoms of Narcissistic Abuse

When the parent's behavior is narcissistic, the child is at risk. This parent is often quick to snap at the child and demands everything, which is unhealthy for the child and can lead to further abuse. The child will also often follow the parent's demands without thinking logically or gaining self-control. This can lead to many issues, including identity crises and loneliness.

Narcissists also need to project an image of perfection. They may manipulate others by threatening them or minimizing their shortcomings. These people often have a hard time dealing with reality. They are easily used and can even deceive friends and loved ones.

Narcissistic abuse is often self-centered, but it can also include physical abuse. The abuser may break things, hurt others, or even use physical violence and intimidation to gain attention. The narcissist's behavior can be frightening and unpredictably impulsive.

When dealing with a narcissistic parent, it is important to know your rights and the limitations of those rights. You cannot expect a narcissistic parent to be able to make decisions about your child's life. But you must be able to communicate your needs and express your feelings without letting the abuser dictate your choices.

Narcissistic parents are often jealous of their children. They constantly compete with their children and will do anything to maintain control over their lives. Whether physical or emotional, narcissists will do everything they can to make their kids feel inferior and unworthy.

There are many red flags a parent should look for if they suspect a narcissistic parent is abusing their child. This abuse can be physical or emotional. In extreme cases, a child may not realize they are being abused until they are adults when those early traumatic experiences seep into their adult relationships. Luckily, there are ways to overcome the trauma and move forward.

If you believe your child is being abused by a narcissist, you need to get help right away. Even if you think you have handled the situation yourself, you might make things worse.

Narcissists are notorious for their lack of respect for boundaries. If you try to set boundaries with the abuser, they may ignore or challenge you. They may even give you the silent treatment until you give in. They will try to regain your trust and sway you back into their orbit by convincing you that it never happened.

Children with narcissistic parents are in a state of constant competition, and they are often jealous of others. Their lack of empathy for others will cause them to seek attention from family and friends constantly.

One of the most important signs of narcissistic abuse is a child's personality change. The child who has been subjected to narcissistic abuse will have a distorted sense of reality, which can lead to severe emotional pain.

- **Narcissistic Abuse Causes Personality Changes in Kids**

Kids whose parents are narcissists are susceptible to the manipulations and control of their narcissistic parents. Their parents are often demanding, and they must acquiesce to their demands. They lack healthy models and can be opposed to healthy boundaries.

Kids of narcissistic parents are likely to experience many changes in their personalities. This is because narcissistic parents are often emotionally abusive and hold their children to unrealistic expectations. This makes the child feel confused and teaches the child a sense of distrust. While narcissism is common, a small percentage of children experience it, and the results can be long-term.

In addition to the emotional and psychological abuse, children of narcissistic parents may have difficulty forming healthy relationships. They may be less open to new relationships, distrust people, and abandon their emotional intimacy. Children who have experienced narcissistic abuse are more likely to experience low self-esteem, codependency, and guilt. Narcissistic kids are also more likely to develop PTSD, a psychological disorder caused by the effects of narcissistic abuse.

- **Narcissistic Abuse Destabilizes the Sense of Reality**

Children who are subjected to narcissistic abuse suffer from destabilized senses of reality. This condition is caused by the fact that they are denied the opportunity to verify and evaluate their reality, a process known as scapegoating. This process involves blaming the victim for the abuse rather than holding the abuser accountable for their behavior.

Narcissists are not only emotionally abusive to children but also hold them to impossible standards and expectations. Children with narcissistic parents may become like extensions of their parents' egos, constantly being asked to act "perfect," although this would be counterproductive.

- **Narcissistic Abuse Makes a Narcissist Feel Guilty**

Children raised by a narcissist develop an insecure and anxious attachment style. They often end up in abusive relationships as adults. They carry a pervasive sense of worthlessness and toxic shame. The narcissist also teaches these children to ignore their needs and cater to others. They also learn to walk on eggshells and avoid public attention and criticism.

It is important to note that narcissists rarely publicly identify themselves as having a personality disorder, so they are often reluctant to treat their children in custody cases. Narcissists may also harass a child's counselor, preventing them from being able to focus on the needs of the child. As a result, the narcissist may use the counselor as a weapon against the non-NPD parent.

- **Narcissistic Abuse Causes Emotional Pain**

A malignant narcissist is a person who has no empathy for anyone but himself. They enjoy the sense of power and control they can gain by harming others. Children who are exposed to this type of abuse experience intense emotional pain.

The psychological toll of narcissistic abuse can be severe, affecting a child's development for years. It can lead to feelings of low self-worth, anxiety, and depression. These symptoms can be life-long, though some survivors have recovered.

A child suffering from narcissistic abuse may question their worth. They may have problems trusting others and feel like they do not belong. They may also have issues with making decisions. They may feel guilty about the abuse, preventing them from seeking help. They may find it hard to make decisions, often due to the narcissist's overbearing.

- **Narcissistic Abuse Causes Chronic Self-Blame**

Children subjected to narcissistic abuse often develop a history of chronic self-blame. These children are taught that they are not good enough for their narcissistic parents, and as a result, they tend to blame themselves for little things like not finishing their homework on time or making small mistakes. This is a sign of chronic self-blame that can persist into adulthood.

Often, children who suffer from narcissistic abuse have low self-esteem, which leads to depression and other mental health problems later in life. Narcissistic parents often expect their children to follow their lead and take their instructions without question. This lack of confidence can even affect a child's ability to form healthy relationships with other people.

Traits of Children of Narcissists

Narcissistic children often display traits of their parents' personalities. They learn to act in unhealthy ways around other people and often live vicariously through them. These patterns are hard to break without the support of family members or professional help. Children of narcissists are likely to blame themselves for even small mistakes, such as not finishing their homework on time. They will constantly focus on what they did wrong instead of what they did right.

Children of narcissists typically have low self-esteem throughout their childhood and into their adulthood. They may feel insecure and incapable of being independent or good enough and may seek solace in drugs or alcohol to compensate for their lack of self-esteem. If this pattern continues, children of narcissists may begin to develop personality changes, including substance abuse.

Children of narcissists lack empathy and cannot identify with other people's feelings. They view other people as objects to serve their needs and can be manipulative and exploit others to that end. They do not care if they are hurting others or themselves in the process.

Narcissistic children have a deep need to be the center of attention. They present themselves as the "Golden Child" in school and can use their natural charms to impress teachers. These kids can be disruptive and cause chaos in the classroom. Their behavior is often reported as behavior problems by their school.

Ways to Report Narcissistic Abuse

There are several ways to prove narcissistic abuse in a child's life. It would be best if you kept calm, as the abuser will try to gaslight you and the abused victim. The first way is to tell a trusted adult or friend about the abuse. Using contemporaneous notes will help you to prove the abuse.

Another way to prove narcissistic abuse is to keep records of the abuse. Write down every conversation, and make sure you document the details. Then, you can challenge the narcissist's version of events.

You can also provide evidence such as text messages, emails, and voicemail messages. But be careful not to use these as evidence against your ex-partner - they could be used against you in court!

Videotaping the abuse will also help. It can also help if the child has other witnesses. However, narcissists may appear to behave properly in public and may not be able to be caught on videotape. However, if you can get witness statements, you are one step closer to proving narcissistic abuse in a child.

Chapter 16:
Parental Alienation - A Form of Emotional Child Abuse

Parental Alienation - What It Is

Parental alienation is a tactic in which one parent deliberately expresses to the child unwarranted animosity toward the other parent. It can be accomplished through manipulation, negative actions, or other means. By manipulating the child's emotions against the other parent, this tactic seeks to sour the child's relationship with that parent.

During a divorce, parental alienation, a particular family dynamic, may occur in which the kid exhibits excessive hostility and rejection toward one parent. It involves at least three parties: the alienating parent, who deliberately and intentionally manipulates the child to reject the other parent; the alienated parent who has been rejected; and the alienated child.

To accomplish their objective, alienating parents employ a range of strategies and techniques, from bad-mouthing and disrupting time spent together to making erroneous accusations of abuse and filing criminal charges. They compel the child to cut ties with the other parent and promote disrespect.

This kind of behavior is considered to be child abuse. Richard Gardner, an American psychiatrist, introduced the word "parental alienation syndrome" (PAS) in 1985. It is the disorder children affected by this psychological abuse have.

According to research, parental alienation occurs in 11% to 15% of divorces. Furthermore, it has been observed that 20% to 25% of parents continue to behave in an alienating way up to 6 years after the divorce.

Parental Alienation - What It Is Not

Parental alienation is the unjustified effort by one parent to destroy their child's relationship with the other parent. A child rejecting a parent for valid reasons, however, does not amount to alienation.

A history of domestic violence, child physical, emotional, or sexual abuse, neglect, mental health issues, or drug abuse are all valid reasons for the child's rejection.

Rejection based on these reasons is an estrangement, not alienation.

Signs of Parental Alienation

Parental alienation, regardless of the terminology or whether it is recognized as a diagnosable disorder, is linked to specific behavioral patterns in both the alienating parent and the alienated child.

- **The Alienating Parent's Behavior**

The following harmful parenting techniques are commonly used by alienating parents.

- Bad-mouthing
- Making the targeted parent seem dangerous
- Involving the child in parental conflict, child support, or custody dispute
- Accusing the targeted parent of not loving the child

- Disparaging the targeted parent in front of the authorities

- Limiting visits, hiding contact information, or keeping the child hidden

- Bringing up the targeted parent's new or extended family in a negative way

- Monitoring the targeted parent's calls and texts

- **The Child's Behavior**

The signs of PAS recognized by Gardner that alienated children frequently exhibit include:

- The targeted parent may be the subject of constant name-calling, criticism, and denigration from the child.

- When questioned, the child gives flimsy, pointless, or ridiculous explanations for their criticism.

- The child asserts that their emotions are their own, not that of the alienating parent.

- The targeted parent is seen by the kid as all-bad, while the alienating parent is seen as all-good. Therefore, regardless of the situation, they favor the alienating parent over the targeted parent.

- Since the child believes that the targeted parent is completely bad, they lack empathy for them and seem to boast about their animosity.

- The child uses the alienating parent's experiences to support their own claims.

Effects of Parental Alienation on Adult Children

Children who experience parental alienation may suffer severe consequences that persist into adulthood. Those include:

- Low self-esteem and self-hatred
- Depression
- Low self-sufficiency
- Insecure attachment style
- Drug and alcohol abuse
- Trust issues
- Alienation from their own children
- Divorce

How to Cope With Parental Alienation

When you finally muster the courage to leave your narcissist, you would have probably lost many things from being in that relationship, including your self-worth, youth, time, money, and sanity. With the help of their deft manipulation techniques, you have seen how your narcissist has persuaded your family and friends that you are the crazy one and they are the victims. People are deceived without even realizing it. You experience feelings of retaliation, anger, revenge, isolation, and humiliation.

Now, you look around you and realize that you are losing your children as well. They are being manipulated and turned against you. How do you deal with that? Below are some tips:

- **Do Not Be Aggressive**
 Keep in mind that you were constantly placed on the defensive throughout the length of your relationship with the narcissist. Do not allow them to keep doing that.

- **Be Persistent**
 Do not succumb to feelings of failure and hopelessness. If you give up and submit to your weakest self, you have no power. The best interests of your children will be met if they sense your strength and do not witness you being used by the other parent.

- **Resist the Urge to Seek Your Children's Approval Because Striving for That Is Never a Good Idea**
 As soon as you depend on your children's approval, you have ceded control to them and the other parent. You must continually validate yourself to achieve this, and you must also receive validation from your secure relationships.

- **Acknowledge That You Are Not Alone**
 Other parents also experience difficulties. Other parents, even those not in narcissistic relationships, experience challenges with their children as well.

- **Have a Positive Outlook**
 For the sake of your health, you must maintain a balanced view. The best method to accomplish this is to think things through with maturity and balance rather than acting on your emotions.

- **Practice Self-Care and Acceptance**
  Do not focus on all the bad things that happened. Narcissists want you to do that. Do not let them ruin your happiness and sanity, even if they can drag your kids into their world of lies and cruelty.

Chapter 17:
Protecting and Making it Easier for Your Child

Solomon's Wisdom Regarding Children

King Solomon of Israel was considered wise regarding children. The Bible recounts a battle for custody of a child between two women. Both claimed to be the child's true mother, so King Solomon declared that the child should be cut in two. One woman agreed, but the child's mother would not and said that the first woman could have the boy; she would not see her child harmed. The wise king realized that the child belonged to the second woman and gave her the child.

If you are worried about your children's future, you should heed the wisdom of Solomon and follow his example. You do not want to risk your children's lives by abusing them or harming them.

Protecting children, especially young children, from harm is your top priority as a parent; you have a legal duty to protect them. However, it is not always simple. There are many aspects to the laws that can make it difficult to protect your child.

When your marriage ends, you are not the only one who is affected; your children are too. If your divorce is final, your children may face a new challenge: being raised by two very different people. While this time is painful for the child, there are many ways to make it easier for both of you.

How to Make It Easier for You and Your Child After Separation

One of the best ways to help your child adjust after separation is to include them in the decision-making process.

It will benefit both parents to continue the routines and traditions they had before the separation. For example, you can organize a family night once a month. You can also plan a game night or a trip to the park.

There are several ways to make it easier for you and the child to reunite after separation. Do not talk negatively about the other parent in front of the child. Similarly, do not involve the child in meetings with attorneys or other adults. While it is important to communicate the details of the separation, be sure to keep it as neutral as possible.

Understandably, you and your ex-partner will have different parenting styles, but remember that your child is going through a major transition. Instead of trying to "convince" the other parent to change their parenting style, make the changes slowly. The children will be more accepting of gradual changes. Avoid letting your ex-partner be the "fun parent" and ignore the rules.

Children need a familiar environment and a consistent daily routine with age-appropriate limits. Try to maintain the same routines for the children in both households. Creating a familiar routine for your children will help them feel secure.

A very good way to help children cope with a separation is to communicate effectively with the other parent. Be aware that children will ask questions and have specific concerns. It is therefore important to reassure them of these things. For example, if they ask when mom will move back, they may worry about not seeing her.

As a parent, make sure your child knows separation is not easy for you. Children may feel withdrawn or isolated and may develop depression or adjustment disorder. They may be unwilling to go to school and may experience depression or even a depressed state. These symptoms can be connected to divorce, so you must be honest with your child and keep your relationship positive.

Parenting With a Child After Separation

If you have separated from your partner, you will need to decide the living arrangements for your children. It would be best if you also decided on your roles as parents.

The two of you should try to maintain a healthy co-parenting relationship. This is a special relationship between separated or divorced parents where both work toward their children's best interests. Be sure to communicate regularly with your ex and ensure that you are on the same page regarding your child's welfare. If possible, avoid arguing with your ex and focus on raising your child.

Validating Your Feelings to the Children

Validation is the act of listening, acknowledging, and accepting another person's experience. It helps children develop emotional intelligence, reduces tantrums, and develops self-compassion. Validating your feelings with your children can help them recognize their feelings and learn to express them more appropriately.

Validating another person's emotions is a powerful way to de-escalate an emotionally charged situation. It allows a child to feel heard and accepted, which helps the child move through a meltdown more quickly. It also helps a child decide what to do next.

Emotional validation builds trust and confidence in children. It teaches them how to regulate their emotions, which is key to healthy psychological development. It also helps them develop coping skills that prevent them from acting out. Children cannot express their needs if they do not feel accepted and understood. Therefore, parents need to be skilled in validating children's feelings.

As a parent, you can validate your child's emotions by being present and providing support when needed. When children feel upset, parents should sit nearby to show that they care and support them. Sitting nearby indicates that you understand them and model how to stay calm in stressful situations.

1- It Helps Build Emotional Intelligence in Children

Teaching children about emotions is one of the keys to developing emotional intelligence. It helps children learn to recognize and relate their feelings to others, which can help prevent them from engaging in unhealthy behavior. One way to help children build emotional intelligence is by reading stories. When your child asks you what a character is feeling, tell them the appropriate emotion. If you are unsure, you can use an age guide to help you determine what your child feels.

Children often feel awkward expressing their feelings, but doing so can help them learn to regulate their own emotions. It can also help them learn to deal with difficult situations in their lives. One of the most important things you can do is validate your child's feelings. By doing this, you will be setting the foundation for positive coping skills in the future.

2- It Reduces Tantrums

Rather than ignoring tantrums, parents should try to validate their children's feelings to lessen the intensity of the behavior and prevent it from becoming explosive. However, it is important to note that validating your feelings does not mean that you should focus on bad behavior. Dismissing bad behavior (called "actively ignoring") will only encourage the child to do it again. Parents should remember that attention is the most powerful tool for influencing children's behavior. Therefore, it is important to focus on the appropriate behaviors and not on the ones that are not.

Providing your child with an outlet for their feelings will make it less likely for them to act out of frustration and disappointment. In addition, this will help prevent the child from feeling embarrassed because they are unsure how to express their feelings. As a result, validating your child's feelings will help them grow their emotional development.

3- It Helps Develop Self-Compassion in Children

As a parent, constructively expressing your feelings and validating your children's feelings is important in helping them develop self-compassion. While offering advice or changing your child's behavior may be tempting, the goal is to allow them to recognize that their feelings are valid.

For example, a child may feel sad because they are unhappy or upset because of a recent setback. In this case, it is okay to offer encouragement to help the child become more accepting of the situation.

Children often cannot articulate their feelings, so it can be challenging to help them learn how to express compassion. Using social stories or emotional cards to model compassionate behavior can help.

4- It Helps Teach Children to Self-Regulate

Teaching your child to recognize and understand their emotions is vital to developing self-regulation. This skill helps kids deal with emotions and avoid emotional outbursts or disruptions. Children need to realize that their feelings are valid and okay. They also need to learn to distinguish between their feelings and behaviors.

While some children naturally have an even temper, most children need support to develop these self-regulation skills. It takes a little time, but they can do it. The first step is to understand your child's fears. If a child is afraid of diving, for example, you might think that they are being overly dramatic, but it is normal for them to feel that way, and it is important to acknowledge the feeling and help your child overcome it.

Tips for Using "I" Statements

Using "I" statements effectively expresses your feelings without putting the other person on the defensive. It allows you to express your feelings and describe your behavior or action. In addition, using "I" statements helps you confidently explain your point of view. Here are some tips for using this powerful technique:

1- Using "I" Statements to Frame Opening Statements

A great opening statement starts with "I." The first sentence should be an affirmation of who you are. Then you should state why you disagree with what the other party is doing. When making this statement, ensure it is connected to what was presented. Then, you can focus on how the other person can help you resolve the situation or prevent it from happening again.

2- Using "I" Statements to Make Requests

Using "I" statements to make requests is an effective way to express your needs and expectations. These statements allow you to express yourself without making others feel defensive. They also help you find a resolution to a problem and prevent similar issues in the future. Use these statements when you disagree with someone. Using "I" statements can prevent you from hurting someone's feelings and causing further misunderstanding.

Before speaking to someone, think about your needs and feelings for a few minutes. Writing them out will help you put your thoughts into words, and it can also be helpful to share them with a supportive friend. It is also important to choose a calm setting when speaking to someone in anger.

Explaining Your Point of View With Confidence

Using "I" statements can help you express your thoughts and feelings without being confrontational. They allow you to tell how you feel and how the actions you are describing are causing stress. They also help you express your point of view without making the other person feel defensive. They can help clarify your point of view if you disagree with what they say.

Chapter 18:
Empathy Parenting - What You Should Know

Empathy Parenting – What You Should Know

Empathy parenting is an important method of raising children, but you should know a few things before applying it. First, remember to acknowledge your feelings and give yourself a minute before you respond. This shows your child that you are trying to understand their point of view and that you are capable of self-control.

Empathy

Research shows that parenting styles with low levels of empathy are less likely to help children meet their needs. Parents with low levels of empathy are more likely to view their children's specific developmental needs as irritating rather than a sign of growth. Developing empathy in parenting, however, benefits children and young people, especially families at risk for child maltreatment.

Empathy in parenting is important because it helps parents connect to their children, who realize their parents have their best interests at heart. It also shows children their parents care for and love them even during difficult times. Ultimately, this builds trust and a strong emotional bond. This connection is important for the development of the child.

To develop empathy in parenting, you must learn to understand your child's feelings. Toddlers are still developing the ability to share and understand their emotions. Embracing all your child's emotions in your life will help them know how to express their feelings. A simple act of holding your toddler when they cry will let them know you understand and care.

Relationship Between Parents and Children

The relationship between parents and children is one of the most important factors affecting the development of empathy. Empathy is an adaptive parenting skill that develops a child's ability to experience emotions in others. This skill is highly developed during toddlerhood and is a critical time to examine parenting influences.

A strong relationship between empathy and parent-child quality is a prerequisite for effective parenting. Parents must encourage empathy by demonstrating remorse after infractions and giving the child a chance to make things right. In addition, parents should avoid excessive guilt and self-deprecation. Empathy in parenting is about showing concern and compassion for others.

Communication problems with children top parents' list of complaints. This is not only painful for parents but also has consequences for children. A close relationship between parent and child is the best predictor of a child's stability and development. An emotionally distant child will not be open to a parent. Furthermore, mistaken empathy for sympathy can lead a child to shut down communication.

- **Influence of Empathy on Child's Behavior**

A study of nearly 4,000 children found a strong correlation between parents' empathy and children's behavior. Children with more empathy from their parents were less likely to engage in risky behaviors and act out in adolescence. The results also showed that the quality of parental empathy is associated with a lower risk of violent and aggressive behavior. However, these findings are not conclusive. Future research must look beyond this simple correlation.

This study was conducted in middle-class European-American families. There was no evidence of racial differences in inhibited temperament; however, some evidence suggests that children from lower socioeconomic backgrounds may be more prone to inhibited temperament than children from middle-class and upper-class European American families. Different cultures may also respond to inhibited temperament differently, so parents in different cultural settings may use different strategies to socialize empathy.

Inhibited temperament and empathy are linked to lower empathy in children with high levels of inhibited temperament. This relationship is consistent with other research on parenting children with high levels of inhibition. This finding suggests that parenting practices traditionally regarded as "adoptive" for children with lower levels of inhibition may be less effective.

- **Influence of Empathy on Child's Self-Confidence**

Empathy parenting is an important component of self-regulation for kids. Taking a moment to acknowledge your emotions and recognize that your child feels stressed or upset is a great way to show your child that you care about his or her feelings. It's also important to model self-control and take your time before responding.

Parents who display empathy are more likely to protect their children from aggression and risky behavior. Similarly, children who felt their parents had empathy for them were less likely to engage in risky behaviors, which supports the theory that parents who show empathy to their children are more likely to support them as they reach adulthood.

Child empathy can be developed in children as young as five. Using theoretical problems and situations to teach children to understand other people's feelings will help them develop this important skill. By the time children reach the age of eight, they will be able to discuss more complex moral dilemmas.

Chapter 19:
Strategies for Healthy Emotional Regulation

Narcissists believe they have failed at life if they do not feel like the best person in the world. They achieve this by making themselves the center of attention at all times. However, they are easily dysregulated and quite insecure. They must hurt you to demonstrate their power over you. A narcissist must dysregulate others to survive.

Narcissists can inflict great emotional harm on individuals they have gaslighted, especially if the victim is at their most vulnerable. The victim is susceptible to believing anything the narcissist says, leading to feelings of guilt, self-doubt, self-criticism, and self-hatred. Nobody is more aware of the narcissist's need to watch others experience emotional breakdowns than you are.

You can, however, learn to manage your thoughts and emotions. Healthy individuals who respect their boundaries and have a strong sense of self do not allow themselves to become involved in these kinds of interactions with others. Use your relationship with your narcissist co-parent as a chance to develop your emotional intelligence and grow into a more resilient person who is not easily influenced by others.

What Is Emotional Regulation?

The emotions you are experiencing are real and normal. Depending on your emotional regulation skills, how you express and act out those emotions may vary.

The capacity to understand, control, and react to your emotions is known as emotional regulation. It involves developing a window of time between experiencing an emotion and responding to it. Taking a moment to gather your thoughts before responding, for instance.

When you do not know how to manage your emotions, they can take control of you and affect the way you interact with people, yourself, and your surroundings as a whole.

When emotions harm your quality of life, you might wish to look into healthy coping mechanisms and practice regulating your emotions.

Why Is Emotional Regulation Important?

Emotional regulation is a crucial technique for maintaining and establishing healthy relationships as well as for mental health.

When you develop this skill, you can:

- Feel emotionally balanced and in control
- Maintain composure in stressful situations
- Better manage stress
- Safeguard significant relationships
- Actively consider others' needs
- Constructively express your needs
- Maintain your professionalism at work
- Refrain from taking things personally

Signs of Emotional Dysregulation

You might exhibit the following symptoms if you are unable to regulate your emotions:

- Sudden mood swings
- Eating disorders
- Crying episodes
- Emotional outburst
- Relationship issues
- Anger, aggressivity, and violence
- Self-harm
- Substance abuse
- Low threshold for frustration

Strategies That Can Help You Regulate Your Emotions

To manage emotions healthily, below are some strategies that may help:

- **Recognize and Reduce Triggers**

Negative emotions are not something you should try to avoid or be frightened of. You also do not have to keep putting yourself in scenarios that make you feel bad.

When you start to experience powerful emotions, start searching for patterns or contributing elements. You should, however, be honest with yourself. Has something made you feel worthless? We frequently experience strong emotions as a result of our ingrained insecurities, especially those that we try to disguise. What is going on around you, and what memories does it evoke for you from the past?

Once you have identified these triggers, you may begin to look into why they have such a strong impact and whether you can lessen it.

- **Pay Attention to Physical Symptoms**

Be mindful of your feelings, particularly whether you are hungry or exhausted. These elements may amplify your feelings and lead you to perceive them with greater intensity. You can alter your emotional reaction if you can resolve the underlying problem (such as hunger or fatigue).

- **Engage in Positive Self-Talk**

Your self-talk might turn negative when your emotions feel overwhelming. You may replace part of this negative talk with encouraging remarks if you approach yourself with compassion. The feelings you are experiencing may be lessened by this change.

- **Choose How to Respond**

Most of the time, you can choose how to react. You probably realize the detrimental effect it is having on your relationships if you tend to lash out at people when you are angry.

The next time you experience fear or anger, remember that you have the power to decide how you want to react. That acknowledgment has tremendous power. Can you think of another response before you lash out? Is it feasible for you to communicate with someone your anger without yelling at them? Try experimenting with different responses to see what happens.

- **Look for Positive Emotions**

People are wired to give negative emotions more importance than positive ones. This is referred to as negative bias.

Happiness, satisfaction, and appreciation are examples of positive emotions that are peaceful. Negative feelings, on the other hand, like rage, fear, and frustration, are heavier emotions that are given more importance.

Making it a practice to reflect on these pleasant moments might increase resiliency and well-being.

- **Practice Mindfulness**

Being in a state of mindfulness is unique. It entails being aware of your present moment. You become more conscious of your feelings when in this state. You pay attention to the sounds, feelings, and visual representations that go along with your emotions.

Being mindful allows you to put some distance between yourself and the way you react, which improves focus, promotes feelings of relaxation and tranquility, and helps regulate negative emotions.

Mindfulness exercises include focused breathing and practicing gratitude.

- **Seek Therapy**

It might be challenging to control your own emotions. It necessitates having a high level of self-awareness. Your ability to control your emotions starts to deteriorate when you are struggling in life. A therapist can teach you more effective self-regulation techniques.

Chapter 20:
Mental Health – The Importance of the Expert

A mental health expert or therapist can help you overcome your problems. This person specializes in helping you work through the issues keeping you from living a normal life. There are several ways to find an expert and get the help you need. Read on to discover some of the most important factors when seeking professional help.

Lessons Learned From a Mental Health Expert

There are many reasons why someone may seek the help of a mental health expert or therapist. One of the most common is someone struggling with a mental illness. One out of five adults in the US will experience some form of mental illness. As a result, there are 46 million people who are managing their mental health daily. Regardless of the reason, therapy can be helpful in several ways.

Getting Help From a Mental Health Expert

Getting help from an expert is critical if you are experiencing mental health issues. These professionals can help you with coping strategies.

They may prescribe medications to help you cope with your symptoms. A mental health expert or therapist can also recommend nutrition and lifestyle changes to promote mental health.

Psychiatrists, psychologists, social workers, and nurse practitioners are all qualified to provide mental health treatment. These professionals usually hold doctoral degrees and can provide individual and group therapy to individuals or groups. Some mental health professionals also offer services in medical settings and schools.

When choosing a mental health expert or therapist, it is important to be clear about what you are looking for. The first visit will be a good time to discuss your goals and ask questions about the treatment you will receive. Be open to answering questions to better your chances of a positive outcome.

Questions to Ask a Mental Health Expert

When beginning a new relationship with a therapist or mental health expert, open-ended questions are a good way to get the ball rolling. Many people have misconceptions about therapy and the way it works. They think that therapists give advice and are like friends or family members.

When talking with a mental health expert or therapist, ask about the kind of therapy they offer and how they approach problems. It is also important to understand how they will measure progress.

Ask about their experience working with specific populations. A therapist with experience treating substance use and obsessive-compulsive disorders may be better equipped to deal with those situations than a therapist who only has experience with depression.

This will help you decide if you want to work with them.

Finding a Mental Health Expert

Choosing the right therapist or mental health expert is important. Fortunately, many of these professionals offer initial consultations so that you can get a feel for their skills and expertise. Some mental health providers even offer these consultations for free, so it is always worth trying out a few different options.

To find a therapist or mental health expert, look for someone with experience treating similar problems. For example, if you are suffering from anxiety, search for a clinical psychologist specializing in that field. Or, if you are dealing with family issues, search for a family therapist or licensed professional counselor with experience working with adolescents. It is also a good idea to get referrals from trusted friends and physicians. Moreover, it is useful to determine whether a therapist is familiar with evidence-based practices. This means that they are using techniques that have been proven effective by controlled studies and published research.

Finding a mental health expert or therapist who meets your needs and preferences is critical. It is essential to choose a therapist to whom you relate. Depending on your needs, you may have to meet with several therapists before you find the one that is right for you.

While the process can seem daunting at first, the process of therapy can be extremely beneficial. By working with a trained professional who understands the complexities of mental health, you can work through your issues and make a positive change in your life.

Chapter 21:
What You Should Learn From This Relationship

It can be difficult and painful to be in a relationship with a narcissist, and even harder to be co-parenting with one. However, it is so important when you are ending a really dysfunctional relationship to be able to kind of self-reflect and learn some important lessons from this experience. Below are a few of them:

- **Know Your Value**
  Despite what they may tell you, it is important to remember your value because narcissists live by making their partners feel inferior and undeserving. Remind yourself that you are worthy of being loved and respected by someone who will see you for the person you truly are.

- **Communication Is Crucial**
  Recognizing each other's points of view and allowing them sufficient room to express themselves without interruption or judgment from either party is the first step in developing healthy communication between two people. Whether one partner is a narcissist or not, our relationship will be healthier the more honestly we express our emotions, frustrations, and desires.

- **Do Not Allow Yourself to Be Manipulated**
  One trait shared by narcissists is their propensity for manipulating others. This trait is crucial in any relationship

dynamic, but it is especially crucial when dealing with someone who has narcissistic tendencies because they frequently try to persuade their partners to accept their point of view while ignoring yours, which can cause long-lasting emotional harm if left unchecked. Because both points should coexist in any healthy relationship, regardless of whether one partner has narcissistic ideals or not, make sure your opinion is heard in any type of interpersonal dynamic.

- **Set Boundaries**
 All relationships need boundaries and narcissists will walk all over yours. Be clear about your boundaries to protect your mental and emotional health. Do not count on people to figure out what they are. People need to be taught by you.

- **Concentrate on Your Recovery**
 It takes time to recover from a narcissistic relationship, but it is possible to heal and move on. Focus on your development and objectives while developing your sense of self-worth and self-compassion.

- **Practice Self-Care**
 Self-care is important because being in a relationship with a narcissist can be detrimental to your mental and emotional health. It is crucial to prioritize your own needs and engage in self-care.

- **Seek Help if Needed**
 Narcissistic relationships can be stressful, so it is essential to ask for help from friends, family, or a therapist who can provide support and advice.

Divorce Is Not the End

Like a marriage, divorcing someone usually has a profound impact on one's life.

From an empty home to meals alone, the entire scenario can bring about a lot of changes. You will develop a co-parenting routine which when you follow can necessitate your first-ever days without your children.

A complex jumble of emotions, ranging from betrayal and sadness to fury or even relief, may come over you as you start to get used to the new structure of your life.

Divorce may, to put it bluntly, upend your life. Remembering that divorce does not signify the end of your life might be helpful as you start to rebuild yourself. It represents a fresh start.

Physical and emotional self-care is a crucial step in your post-divorce journey. Below are some tips that will help:

- **First and Foremost, Love Yourself**
  Simply said, you must first love yourself before you can love another person. There is never a better moment than the present to take care of yourself and your needs. Keep in mind that in this situation, the proverb "selfless people are selfish" is valid. It is crucial to take care of your mental and physical needs first since they have an impact on how you later behave as a partner or spouse.

- **Get in Touch With Yourself**
  Even if you believed you knew yourself very well, divorce may cause you to reevaluate who you are. There is no disputing that relationships may alter a person, and you could find that

you are not entirely the same person you were before getting married.

According to your personal likes, dislikes, and favored habits, some of your present behaviors and tastes may have developed spontaneously, while some may be a reflection of your ex's preferences. Perhaps you would prefer (or would not prefer) to spend more time outdoors than in a gym, live in the countryside than in the city, or eat healthier.

After your divorce, you should set out on your own journey. As you go, take some time along the way to reflect on your needs and how you may meet them.

- **Reassess Your Goals**
  It is a great chance to reevaluate your goals, now that you have started a new stage of your life. Are you happy with your career? Should you improve some skills? Are you doing the activities and hobbies you love? What is on your bucket list?

- **Spend Quality Time With Your Children**
  It can be easier to adjust after a divorce if you make it a point to engage in enjoyable activities and establish new traditions with your kids.

  No matter how hectic and demanding your new daily schedule becomes, set aside time each day to check in with your kids and unwind as a family.

- **Connect With Your Loved Ones**
  Your ability to handle the ongoing stress of the divorce and your general well-being can both be greatly improved by

talking to your support network and letting these emotions out.

Friends and relatives can listen sympathetically (and with understanding if they have already gone through a divorce) and provide both emotional support and practical answers, such as where to stay, assistance with the children, or just considerate advice.

- **Expect to Lose Some Friends, but Make New Ones**
  It is very natural to lose some mutual friends after a divorce. Making new acquaintances can foster opportunities for social connection and reduce feelings of loneliness. You can join the gym, take an art class, or volunteer in an organization. You can even join a divorce support group. All those will help you meet people and start new friendships.

- **Date When You Feel Ready**
  When it comes to dating after a divorce, you cannot please all your family and friends. Some will try to pressure you into moving on quickly and dating, while others will think you are moving very fast when they see you with someone.

Recovery does not occur in a straight line. You get to set the rules for your life. There is no ideal window of time for when you are prepared to date once more. Do what feels right for you and trust your gut.

Conclusion

Divorcing a narcissist is not always easy and often ends in a toxic way. To successfully co-parent with a narcissist, you must learn how to deal with their character flaws and the issues around them. Although many believe that you are free from their manipulations and abuse after a divorce, it is not the case if you have a child.

Also, it would be best if you healed before you can co-parent your narcissistic ex in a toxic divorce. The healing process has different stages, and the deep wound your ex has caused may take an extended time before you heal because healing is a deep word of the mind.

Many people mistake recovery for healing, and they are two different things. You can engage in the no-contact method to recover, but you will not heal. There will still be a lot of negative emotions and pressure that have been built up in your heart. You will be burdened and mentally unstable, and each time you meet with them to discuss your kids, your emotions will be close to the surface.

You may choose to stay away completely, but for the sake of your children, you need to reconsider because research has proven to us that one single parent cannot raise a healthy child.

The kids still love your ex and see them as part of the family. They see you as part of the family as well. Therefore, you should not stay away completely after divorce. Your children need your attention more at that stage than when you were married.

There are different cycles of narcissistic abuse because it often does not begin just after you meet these people. At first, they will be the perfect companion, full of surprises, and appear ideal. Then, once you commit yourself, they will start unmasking themselves. When you confront them, they will use their weapons against you.

One of the most potent weapons used by narcissists is verbal abuse. They will insult you and call you names to wound your ego and make you feel worthless. You will doubt everything for which you stand, meaning that you will have to rediscover yourself all over again in your healing process. After all, they will rob you of your fulfillment and make you feel empty.

Covert narcissists, on the other hand, will be openly dramatic for everyone to see. They will publicly disgrace and embarrass you to destroy your ego and make you feel inferior to them. They are highly toxic people. They want attention and applause, and everything revolves around all these. If you are going to co-parent effectively with them, you need to play by the rules and not by their rules.

They are chaotic and destructive attention seekers, and even after divorce, since it is a toxic divorce, they will still have the urge to retaliate and get in your way. They will want to frustrate you at every opportunity they get. Still, you are doing what you are doing because of your children, and you will learn to overlook and be patient. Therefore, healing is crucial in your co-parenting journey.

Some even abandon their children and leave their ex to handle the fallout and have the time to seek the attention they desire and live the exotic life they have always wanted. Narcissists are cheats, manipulators, liars, and proud people. Even after divorce, they will still try to manipulate your emotions to ensure every decision suits their needs.

Remember, you are doing everything for your children's sake, so as much as you can, never enter into an argument with them in front of the kids. Avoid talking or discussing any topic that will result in a fight. Your children's mental health is crucial, and you need them to stay sane. Arguing with your narcissistic ex will further damage their emotions. Always act as though you have heard, but find another way to handle the issues instead.

It would be best if you always made decisions about the kids, their school and education, medical attention and treatment, outings, and events. If any situation you think will not be favorable for the children, ensure you let the other parent know.

Update your ex on everything that pertains to them, and never leave anything out if anything bad happens. They will blame you for not giving the necessary information and for creating a communication gap.

Also, you must be flexible in the co-parenting process. Do not make things difficult for your ex, even if they make mistakes. When they return the children late, never insist on deducting from the number of hours they will spend next time to get back at them. Also, ensure you keep records for future sake. In a situation where your narcissistic ex wants to attack, you will have evidence to show for it.

In conclusion, never bad-mouth your ex in front of the children; it is passing a certain message to them that you both never loved each other, and the children may grow cold around the other parent. Ultimately, you will lose your children's respect, and they will pull away from you. Respect your ex in front of your kids.

Respect their closeness, and do not seek ways to win them over. You are both involved, and you need their contributions in co-parenting. Yours is to satisfy your children and make them happy around you. You can record your conversations with your ex for evidence's sake but respect them. Do not eavesdrop or record their conversations with other people.

You should always ensure that you reach a consensus or have a mutual agreement regarding the children. You can shift ground for your ex if they are not willing to accept your terms, and that is if you are comfortable with their suggestions because narcissists are selfish and always want everything to be in their favor.

Having a mutual agreement is very important in co-parenting. Even before you take any disagreement to court, ensure you have both discussed well enough on that subject matter. You are also teaching your children about effective communication. So, learn the skill and use it to avoid an argument with your ex in co-parenting. You can do active listening more than you speak. It will help you a lot.

When you do the listening more than you talk, you will not always be trapped in one corner by your narcissistic ex during conversations and discussions with them. Always weigh your options before taking any step, and learn to ignore them more than respond to them. This will be helpful in your co-parenting.

Co-parenting can be effective only if you learn the right strategies. Many see it as difficult, but it can become the easiest thing to do after divorce with the right knowledge. Focus on your children and your growth as well. Do the ones you can and allow your ex to do their part and raise healthy children with courage and compassion.

Author's Note

Dear reader,

I hope you enjoyed my book.

Please don't forget to toss up a quick review on Amazon, I will personally read it! Positive or negative, I'm grateful for all feedback.

Reviews are so helpful for self-published authors and your feedback can make such a difference for my book!

Thanks very much for your time, and I look forward to hearing from you soon.

Sincerely,

Melanie

Printed in Great Britain
by Amazon